Guillermo Arriaga won a ~~~~~~~~~~~~~~~~~~~~~ Spain's
National Institute of Fine Arts (INBA) in 1987. In 1991 he published his first novel, *Relato de los esplendores y miserias del Escuadrón Guillotina y de cómo participó en la leyenda de Francisco Villa* (*A Tale of the Splendors and Miseries of the Guillotine Squadron and How It Contributed to the Legend of Francisco Villa*). His second novel, *Un Dulce Olor a Muerte* (*A Sweet Smell of Death*), was published in 1994, and the English translation will be published by Faber and Faber. In 1998 Arriaga wrote the script for a screen adaptation, directed by Gabriel Retes. In 1999 he published both a novel (*El Búfalo de la Noche*) and a volume of stories (*Retorno 201*), while his original screenplay *Amores Perros* was filmed under the direction of Alejandro González Iñárritu.

AMORES PERROS

Guillermo Arriaga

Translated by
Alan Page

faber and faber

First published in 2001
by Faber and Faber Limited
3 Queen Square London WC1N 3AU

Photoset by Faber and Faber Ltd
Printed in England by Mackays of Chatham plc, Chatham, Kent

All rights reserved

© Guillermo Arriaga, 2001
Photos © Optimum Releasing, 2001

Guillermo Arriaga is hereby identified as author of this work in accordance
with Section 77 of the Copyright, Designs and Patents Act 1988

*This book is sold subject to the condition that it shall not, by way of trade or
otherwise, be lent, resold, hired out or otherwise circulated without the publisher's
prior consent in any form of binding or cover other than that in which it is
published and without a similar condition including this condition being imposed
on the subsequent purchaser*

A CIP record for this book
is available from the British Library

ISBN 0-571-21415-0

2 4 6 8 10 9 7 5 3 1

CONTENTS

INTRODUCTION: STRUCTURE AND
CHARACTER IN *AMORES PERROS*

I have always been obsessed by automobile accidents. I find them the most terrible price man pays for technology, for wanting to go beyond his natural limits. An accident is a mixture of speed, blood and twisted metal. They often radically change the victims' lives, not only because of the injuries they may sustain, but also the fears, contrasting emotions and nightmares that remain. Also, a crash can put us in touch with people we would not know otherwise. In a few brutal seconds, they join victims, witnesses, policemen, doctors. They are fortuitous roads for encounters.

I suffered a serious accident on the highway many years ago. On a hunting trip, we turned over into a ravine. I was asleep on the back seat and was awakened by the thud of the truck, after falling three meters, against some rocks. Then we started to roll over and over. The glass breaking, the metal splitting, the truck spiraling downwards, the crunch of bones. The truck stopped. There was a brief silence. Then the screams, the radiator steam escaping and the cries for help.

Miraculously, we all survived, saved by the metal coolers we were carrying tied to the roof. The script for *Amores Perros* stems from a car crash for two main reasons: first, to carry the characters to an extreme situation; and second, because it leads to the meeting of dissimilar characters. However, the crash is not the script's marrow. It is, so to speak, the catalyst that accelerates or modifies the characters' existence.

When I was younger I read *The Sound and the Fury* by William Faulkner. I was fascinated by how he handled time and his characters' point of view. I discovered the importance of subjugating the structure to the story to be told. He made me realize that every story exhales its own narrative breath. I kept reading Faulkner. Every novel was told differently – *The Wild Palms, Absalom, Absalom!, Light in August, As I Lay Dying*. In each one a fiercely human story was told, without any complacencies, deep, terrible and hopeful at the same time.

I then became interested in bringing a similar structure to the movies – one that was subordinate to the story and not vice versa. I wanted to write a script that showed us the story of a car crash, the story of the present and future. What led to this accident? What happened during the accident? What were its consequences?

This was the initial position for *Amores Perros*, but as I said, the accident could not be the main part of the script. I wanted my characters to be involved in love stories; that love itself was what drove them to extremes and took them to situations where they had to make vital and intense decisions; that love represents pain and hope. The crossroads between life and death.

I wanted stories of forbidden love, where loving presupposed a risk and an adventure. It is surprising that a feeling as noble as love can become such a destructive force. Thus the Spanish title *Amores Perros*. Love that bites, that devours. Intense, fierce, brave and fearsome. Love put to the test, love at the edge of the abyss.

The three stories of *Amores Perros* implicitly reflect on father figures. In all three, the parents are absent or lost. In the first story there is no father and the brothers fight over an empty throne; in the second a father abandons his family; and in the third a disappeared father tries to return to the world he has lost.

Why absent fathers? Freud's thesis, posited in *Totem and Taboo*, seems to be truer than ever today: disappeared fathers and brothers destroying themselves. Authority figures have become evanescent and have given way to figures of power. This is true if authority is understood to be that which appears naturally by conviction, charisma, wisdom or experience, and power as that which is obtained through bureaucracy, institutions or sheer strength. This substitution of authority for power has led to the loss of a fundamental value: fraternity. As human beings we are reaching intolerable levels of violence. Respect for the other is lost. Whoever is different to me becomes my enemy, be it by race, religion or social class. Proof of this is the horrors of the war in Bosnia and Kosovo, the Tutsis and the Hutus, and violent crime in large cities. There is no guiding authority to bring dialogue and consensus.

In *Amores Perros*, two stories deal with confrontations between brothers. This is not the fight between Cain and Abel. It is Cain against Cain. Humans against humans, dogs against dogs. Brotherhood broken.

It was very important to me for the characters in *Amores Perros* to behave paradoxically, to be contradictory. I wanted them to say one thing and do another, to look for good through evil, to construct by destroying, to love by hating. I find that paradoxical characters are the ones that most seduce the audience. They are the ones who most reveal the human condition. Morals try to guide us toward absolute concepts: yes and no, right and wrong, one and the other. Life is relative, that is why it is paradoxical.

'Good' and 'bad' characters bore me. Characters that are debated hour after hour are far more interesting: those that come near the abyss and feel vertigo, but do not fall; those that are capable of being who they are and fighting for what they believe in until the end, only to discover that the paradise they expected was nonexistent. Characters that are not ruined despite having been defeated for a long time.

One of the most frightening evils of contemporary society is the abominable 'political correctness' – the absolute dilution of human relations (perhaps the most devastating form of violence). Everything takes on a hypocritical, 'nice' tone. Everything tends to be aseptic, lacking in depth and intensity – to be civilized. Ralph Waldo Emerson said that the human race would disappear by excess of civilization. Human beings bound by unpolluted, castrating morals. Ecologists forget that the most important nature to be defended is human nature.

I have tried to keep the characters in *Amores Perros* consistent with their nature. If the frog and scorpion anecdote had not been already used in *The Crying Game*, I would have used it at some point in the script. That is: a scorpion asks a frog to carry him across the river on his back. The frog refuses: 'You might sting me and kill me.' The scorpion answers, 'No, if I sting you and you die, so do I since I don't know how to swim.' The frog accepts. In the middle of the river the scorpion stings the frog. The dying frog looks at the scorpion: 'Why did you do it? Now we'll both die.' The scorpion, sinking, answers, 'It's my nature.' This is what I wanted the script to reflect: characters that sink under the weight of their own nature and do not regret it.

I wanted to write a script as far away as possible from anything politically correct. I was not interested in a lesson in morality. I wanted to show characters in all their pain, joy, faith, kindness and cruelty. Characters in very basic human situations: betrayal, love, abandon, hate, struggle. Ethical judgments had to come from the spectator, not from the film. Although this, we know, is an illusion: implicit in every aesthetic is an ethic.

I feel the characters are revealed through the decisions they make. In existentialist terms: living is choosing. But I also wanted these characters to be permeated by the worlds their decisions left behind. Sometimes our deepest nostalgias have more to do with what we do not experience rather than what we do. We carry the skin we never touched on our fingertips, the fights we never fought on our knuckles, in our heart what we left behind. In *Amores Perros*, Susana stays with Ramiro, Daniel with Valeria and el Chivo decides to return. They have decided, but their lives are marked by what they abandon.

The script posits a synthesis: the life of a man divided into three characters – a boy under twenty, a man of forty and a man of sixty. One's problems might very well be another's. And these three characters end their stories similarly: the three discover who they are and become themselves. They discover that pain is also a path toward hope. It is in these conclusions that the three characters converge.

I chose the dogs as a metaphor for what happens to these characters. In the first story, Cofi, a docile home dog, turns into a destructive fighting dog, just like Octavio, who becomes a murderer. In the second story, Richi, the little Maltese dog, is lost under the hardwood floor – a metaphor for the hell Daniel and Valeria live through above and Valeria's rotting leg. In the third story, Cofi reveals to el Chivo his own condition – that of a killer. Dog redeems man. Through Cofi, el Chivo discovers who he is and how low he has fallen. From then on he will try to recover and regain his daughter's lost love for him.

Choosing dogs was not only because of a personal predilection (I couldn't have chosen cats – I don't like them), but because I believe this is the animal with which we have the strongest ties. It is the species we have shared the most with and which most allows us to understand ourselves. The dog we own says a lot about who we are, from one who gleefully accepts his dog's bestiality, to those who try to disguise it with vests, bowties and haircuts. In *Amores Perros*, we know the characters largely because of the dog they have.

My relationship with Alejandro González Iñárritu, the film's director, was fundamental. I would get together with him once a week while I was writing. He would ask questions, make suggestions, criticize and impel me forward. He brought out the best in me and thanks to him this script achieved what it did. This script owes a lot to him. He then let me do the same while he was filming. He invited me to the rehearsals and the set, and I suggested and commented. We broke the paradigm that the writer and director are enemies. We worked in mutual respect and harmony with tremendous complicity. The way it should be, I suppose.

I must also acknowledge the work of our executive producers, Martha Sosa and Francisco González Compeán, and of the directors of Altavista Films, Alejandro Soberón and Federico González Compeán. They were respectful of our work, suggested changes to the script (but did not impose them) and put their money into a risky, unconventional film. They trusted and supported us, two virtues hard to find in film producers.

I hope the characters and stories in *Amores Perros* touch the hearts and entrails of many people. That is what films are for. Or at least, that is why I write them.

Guillermo Arriaga
Translated by Alan Page

Amores Perros was premièred in May 2000 at the Cannes Film Festival, where it was awarded the Grand Prize of the International Critics' Week.

MAIN CAST

EL CHIVO	Emilio Echevarría
OCTAVIO	Gael García Bernal
VALERIA	Goya Toledo
DANIEL	Alvaro Guerrero
SUSANA	Vanessa Bauche
LUIS	Jorge Salinas
RAMIRO	Marco Pérez
GUSTAVO	Rodrigo Murray
JORGE	Humberto Busto
MAURICIO	Gerardo Campbell
TÍA LUISA	Rosa María Bianchi
MAMA SUSANA	Dunia Saldívar
MAMA OCTAVIO	Adriana Barraza
LEONARDO	José Sefami
MARU	Lourdes Echevarría
JULIETA	Laura Almela
ANDRÉS SALGADO	Ricardo Dalmacci
JAROCHO	Gustavo Sánchez Parra

MAIN CREW

Producer and Director	Alejandro González Iñárritu
Written by	Guillermo Arriaga
Executive Producers	Francisco González Compeán
	Martha Sosa
Director of Photography	Rodrigo Prieto
Production Designer	Brigitte Broch
Wardrobe Designer	Gabriela Diaque
Sound Designer	Martín Hernández
Music	Gustavo Santaolaya

EXT. STREET — DAY

It's midday. Sunny. A silver 1987 VW Rabbit speeds through the streets.

INT. CAR — DAY

Inside the car are Octavio and Jorge, both sixteen years old. They have long hair and jeans. Octavio is wearing a leather jacket. Jorge looks older; although Octavio's face reveals a slight naivety, his eyes are more penetrating.

A strong black dog of indefinite breed lies in the back of the car, bleeding profusely from his side.

Octavio drives while Jorge repeatedly turns around to take care of the dog.

OCTAVIO

Are they still coming?

Jorge turns to look back.

JORGE

I don't know, I don't see them.
(*still turning*)
Step on it, here they come.

Octavio turns on an avenue and a white Topaz catches up to them.

Step on it, step on it . . .

Octavio shifts from third to second gear and floors the accelerator. The persecution goes on through many streets. Both are nervous. A truck cuts across before them.

Watch out!

Octavio breaks violently and the dog slips on to the floor. Jorge tries to hold him and coats his hands in blood.

1

OCTAVIO

Is he dead?

Jorge doesn't answer as he tries to pick the animal up.

Dammit! Is he dead?

JORGE

No, no . . .

Octavio looks into the rear-view mirror. The Topaz is closing in. He accelerates. Jorge cannot lift the dog because of the speed they are driving at. With a risky manoeuvre, Octavio turns the wrong way up a narrow one-way street and manages to shake off his persecutors.

OCTAVIO

Suckers!

They breathe agitatedly, sweat. Jorge manages to lift the dog on to the seat. Octavio dodges two or three cars driving toward him and turns on to another avenue. Jorge checks the animal's wound: it is oozing a great deal of blood. He takes off his shirt and covers the wound. The dog groans. Jorge pets it to calm it down.

Octavio turns to look at the dog. When he turns around again to look in the rear-view mirror he discovers the Topaz has caught up with them again.

Fuck!

EXT. STREET — DAY

Octavio floors the accelerator again. The Topaz drives up next to them. There are three men in it. The man in the back seat pulls out a gun and points it at them. Octavio turns violently, passes a bus on its right and leaves them behind. The stoplight turns red. Just when it looks like the Rabbit is going to make it, a gold Honda Accord crosses the intersection and they ram it on its right side.

The Rabbit spins out of control and tumbles. The smashed Accord rolls on and crashes into the sidewalk. The Rabbit lands wheels-up on to the divider.

TITLE OVER BLACK SCREEN: 'BLACK DOG'

INT. HOUSE — DAY

The camera goes down the hallway of a working-class house. In a corner there is a man stroking a bull terrier strapped into a muzzle. On the opposite corner some men are tending to a bleeding dog. It is an arena made of green wooden planks.

In the middle of the arena is Mauricio, a fat man with a pleasant face dressed in a sky blue shirt and cashmere pants. He is talking to a thin, long-haired man. He turns to the arena, where el Jarocho, a twenty-eight-year-old man with gulf-coast facial features and curly hair, is taking the muzzle off a German shepherd. Some men cover the last dog's blood with sand.

MAURICIO

Ready?

El Jarocho assents.

How much are you going to put down?

JAROCHO

10,000.

Mauricio turns to a fifty-year-old man who is holding back a ferocious Doberman on the other side of the arena.

MAURICIO

So? Are you in with ten?

The other man nods. Both take out a bundle of bills, which the long-haired man takes.

They're in with ten, they're in with ten, ten on Pancho, ten on Turco.

(*to the owners*)

Psych 'em.

The owners begin to rouse their dogs; they bark furiously. Jorge can be seen among the awestruck audience surrounding the arena. Mauricio opens his arms, sending the dogs into their corners. He gets behind the boards and joins his hands.

3

Let them go.

FADE OUT.

FADE IN TO EXT. OCTAVIO'S HOUSE — DAY

Susana, sixteen years old, wife to Ramiro and sister-in-law to Octavio, gets home dressed in her high-school uniform. She opens the garage door, and the black dog from the first scene pushes it open. Susana sticks out her knee to try and stop it from escaping, but the dog bolts.

> SUSANA
>
> Cofi, Cofi, come here . . .

The dog pays no attention. After about twenty meters he stops to urinate. Susana runs behind him, but the dog escapes again.

> Goddamn dog!

She walks in.

INT. HOUSE — DAY

Susana heads to the dining room. A ten-month-old baby is sitting on a baby chair. Ramiro's mother is in the kitchen.

> SUSANA
>
> Hello, ma'am.
>> *(she picks the baby up)*
> How's he doing?

> MOTHER
>
> Better. He doesn't have a fever any more.

Busy, the mother takes some pots off the burners.

> Susana, I can't take care of Rodrigo tomorrow.

> SUSANA
> *(disconcerted)*
>
> Why?

> MOTHER
>
> I've got to go to the market and then I promised I'd go help my sister with the moving.

SUSANA

Please, help me out, I've got my math final tomorrow . . . I'll
iron tonight if you want . . .

MOTHER

Tell your mother to take care of him . . .

SUSANA
(*sarcastic*)

My mother?

(*shakes her head*)

Please, ma'am, take care of him this week and then I'll sort it
out . . .

MOTHER

No, dear, I've already taken care of mine, now you take care
of yours . . .

The mother walks out to set the table. Susana looks at her, worried.

EXT. STREET — DAY

*El Chivo, a fifty-six-year-old man, tall, tough, with yellow eyes and a
fierce stare, walks the streets with a pushcart followed by five dogs. He
stops to explore a garbage can, rummages and takes out some scraps of
food, which he gives to his dogs.*

INT. GARAGE — DAY

*The people stare awestruck at the fighting dogs. The sound of the growls
and gnashes is terrible. The German shepherd gains the upper hand
and the Doberman falls to the floor, bloodied. Mauricio walks up to the
Doberman's owner.*

MAURICIO

So, what's the deal, do we keep going?

The owner nods.

Man, they're going to kill him.

OWNER

No, man, he'll get right back in it, you'll see.

Mauricio laughs mockingly.

EXT. STREET — DAY

Daniel Estrada, a forty-five-year-old man with big hands, drives a 1996 Stratus. With him are his wife, Julieta, and his eleven- and thirteen-year-old daughters, Lina and Jimena. Julieta is forty years old and good-looking; she has aged well. Traffic is slow. The girls fight.

LINA

Mom, Jimena took my tiara.

JULIETA

Give it back.

JIMENA

It's my tiara.

LINA

No it isn't, I got it as a present.

JIMENA

Liar, I bought it at the supermarket with my money.

JULIETA

Jimena, give it to her, you never use it.

JIMENA

Awww!

She returns it to Lina. They stop at the light. Daniel looks at a billboard. Some workers are putting up an ad with a beautiful model in a miniskirt (Valeria). We can see the slogan: 'Enchant: the way you are'.

JULIETA

When's the magazine coming out?

DANIEL

If everything works out, May the second.

Lina calls out to her mother again.

LINA

Mom! Jimena took my tiara again.

JULIETA
(*turns around, angry*)
Give it back, God dammit!

Daniel looks at them through the rear-view mirror. He looks back at the billboard and stares at Valeria for a few seconds. The light turns green and Daniel drives on.

INT. DINING ROOM

Susana is feeding the baby some pap. The mother is in the kitchen. Octavio walks in and kisses his mother.

OCTAVIO
What's up, Mom . . .

Busy with her chores, she barely responds to the kiss.

MOTHER
Have a seat.

Octavio heads to the dining room and pets the baby's head.

OCTAVIO
Hey, kid.
(*to Susana*)
How's he doing?

SUSANA
Better.

The mother comes in with a plate of minced meat. She serves Octavio and he sits down.

OCTAVIO
Did you know that in Guadalajara, when babies are born, the doctors stick a finger up their ass?

SUSANA
What for?

OCTAVIO
To know what they're going to be when they grow up. Look: if the boy starts screaming, he's going to be a mariachi; if he

7

starts kicking, he's going to be a football player; and if he
starts giggling, he's going to be a faggot.

Susana shakes her head at the joke.

SUSANA
And if it's a girl, then what do you do?

OCTAVIO
We stick our finger in till they're eighteen.

MOTHER
(annoyed)
Octavio, stop talking nonsense.

*Susana starts feeding the baby again. Ramiro walks in. He is a tall,
strong, handsome nineteen-year-old with a tattoo on his right forearm.
He is wearing the red uniform of a supermarket cashier.*

RAMIRO
Susana, did you spill chlorine on my uniform? Just look at it.
(he shows her the stains)
And what about Cofi? Where is that fucking dog?

SUSANA
How about a hello?

RAMIRO
Where?

SUSANA
I don't know.

She nervously lowers her eyes and looks at the Gerber jar.

MOTHER
(to Ramiro)
Have a seat.

Ramiro pays no attention. He stares fixedly at his wife.

RAMIRO
He got away from you again, didn't he, you fucking idiot.

Susana keeps her eyes down.

How many times have I told you to stick out your knee when you open the door so the dog won't get out? How many?

OCTAVIO

Why don't you relax?

RAMIRO

You stay out of this.

OCTAVIO

I don't know why you're making such a fuss if you don't give a shit about the dog. I'm the one that feeds him, walks him . . .

RAMIRO
(*in his face*)
You-stay-out-of-this, this is between me and my wife.

OCTAVIO

Besides, he got away from me, so stop fucking bothering her.

MOTHER
(*to Octavio*)
Weren't you just told to stay out of this?

OCTAVIO

It's just that . . .

MOTHER

Be quiet.

Octavio shuts up. Ramiro points at him with his index finger, threateningly. Susana looks at him, grateful.

EXT. STREET — DAY

El Chivo stops at various garbage cans. His dogs follow him.

INT. GARAGE — DAY

Mauricio puts some bills in el Jarocho's hand.

MAURICIO

Here's your money minus 500 for my commission. That's ten fights undefeated, huh?

9

JAROCHO

Pure fucking luck, fat man.

> (*he takes his money*)

See you Saturday.

MAURICIO

See you.

Jarocho walks out followed by a group of friends. Pancho is on a leash without his muzzle. The Doberman owner drags his dead dog by one leg, takes the collar off and leaves the carcass in the arena.

Hey! Take your dog.

OWNER

You can barbecue him for lunch, for all I care.

He walks away looking at Mauricio scornfully. Mauricio calls a chubby boy that looks like him who has been watching the fight.

MAURICIO

Champiñon, drag that dog out of here.

The boy obeys. He takes the dog by one leg and pulls him out of the arena.

EXT. STREET – DAY

El Jarocho walks out with Pancho. The German shepherd is furious, still fierce from the fight. He tries to attack the bull terrier we saw earlier. El Jarocho can barely control him. He is followed by Alvaro, Chispas, Javier and Jorge.

JAROCHO

The fucking dog's still pissed off . . .

ALVARO

I know, man. The Doberman didn't put up much of a fight.

They try to get him up on to the back of a 1993 Ford pick-up, where there are three cages: one with a Rottweiler, another with a pit bull and an empty one. Pancho resists. In the distance, on the corner, are el Chivo's five dogs. He is nowhere to be seen.

CHISPAS

Why don't you let him have a shot at those dogs? Maybe it'll
calm him down.

JAROCHO

Yeah.

*He leads Pancho toward the corner and riles him up. The dog growls. El
Chivo's dogs mill around, frightened. When el Jarocho is about to let
Pancho loose, el Chivo appears. Upon seeing the furious dog, he takes a
machete from his pushcart and brandishes it threateningly.*

(*to Chispas*)

Let's find him some other fight.

*They turn toward the truck. Pancho is furious. He pulls on his leash
every which way. Suddenly Alvaro points at Cofi on the opposite sidewalk.*

ALVARO

Look, your Tyson's got a rival.

JAVIER

He's a sitting duck.

JORGE

Don't fuck around, that's Octavio's dog.

JAVIER

Exactly . . .

*Jarocho looks at him mockingly and smiles. He brings Pancho within a
few meters of Cofi. He riles him up and lets him go. Pancho bolts off to
attack.*

FADE OUT.

SFX: Dog yelp over black.

INT. OCTAVIO'S HOUSE — DAY

Octavio is lying on his bed watching TV. Someone knocks on his door.

OCTAVIO

Who is it?

SUSANA
(*barely opening the door*)

Can I come in?

OCTAVIO
(*sits up*)

Yeah, come in.

Susana walks in and sits on the bed next to him.

SUSANA

Thanks . . .

OCTAVIO

What for?

SUSANA

For the whole Cofi thing.

Octavio is about to say something when he notices Susana has blood on her earlobe.

OCTAVIO

What happened?

He points at her ear. Susana touches it. She realizes she's bleeding.

SUSANA

Nothing.

OCTAVIO

Did Ramiro do this to you?

SUSANA

He didn't mean to.

OCTAVIO

He didn't mean to?

SUSANA

You know what your brother is like.

OCTAVIO

You shouldn't put up with this, Susana. He treats you like shit.

SUSANA
(*mumbling*)

Not all the time.

OCTAVIO

Sometimes I can't tell if you really are stupid or you're just pretending.

INT. DANIEL ESTRADA'S HOUSE – DAY

Daniel and his daughters walk into the house. The phone rings. Lina runs to pick it up.

LINA

Hello . . . hello . . . hello . . .

Hangs up.

DANIEL

Who was it?

LINA

I don't know. They hung up.

JULIETA

The silent guy again, huh?

Daniel shrugs his shoulders.

Or is it a silent woman?

Daniel doesn't say anything, looks at his watch and walks up the stairs. The phone rings again.

DANIEL
(*yelling*)

I'll answer . . .

Julieta answers in the downstairs hallway.

JULIETA

Hello . . . hello . . .

Hangs up. Daniel looks down the stairwell.

They hung up again.

INT. OCTAVIO'S HOUSE — DAY

Susana and Octavio are lying on the bed, watching TV. The mother knocks on the door and enters.

MOTHER

Octavio, there's someone at the door for you.

OCTAVIO
(*to Susana*)

Hang on a second.

He gets up and walks out. In the hallway, his mother reproaches him.

MOTHER

You know Ramiro doesn't like it when Susana is in your room . . .

OCTAVIO

We were watching television . . .

MOTHER

I don't care what you were doing. Your brother doesn't like it and neither do I. No more, you hear me? N-o m-o-r-e.

Octavio ignores her and walks downstairs. Jorge is waiting for him at the garage door.

OCTAVIO

Hey, man, what's up?

JORGE
(*excited*)

Have you heard?

OCTAVIO

What?

JORGE

Your dog, man, it killed Pancho, el Jarocho's German shepherd.

OCTAVIO

What happened?

JORGE

Jarocho lets Pancho loose on Cofi. When Cofi sees him coming he pulls back and – blam! – he grabs him by the neck and
kills him.

OCTAVIO

What about Cofi?

*Jorge points at the street. Cofi walks calmly along. Octavio whistles and
the dog hurries toward him. Octavio hugs him and checks him out.*

He doesn't even have a scratch.

JORGE

No, man, the other dog didn't even touch him.

Suddenly Jarocho and his friends arrive in the truck. They get out.

JAROCHO

What's up, Octavio?

Octavio answers by moving his head.

You heard about the shit your dog stirred up?

OCTAVIO

Yeah, I just heard.

JAROCHO

What d'you think?

OCTAVIO

Good, huh? Cool.

JAROCHO

Cool?

Octavio nods.

Well, it looks pretty shitty to me.
			(*to his friends*)
Bring out Pancho.

*The friends get up on the back of the pick-up truck and throw Pancho
on to the sidewalk.*

Look what he did to my dog.

Cofi growls at the carcass.

This animal was worth at least 20,000 pesos.

OCTAVIO

You should stuff him. He'd look good in your living room.

JAROCHO

Don't try and be funny, you fucking punk. You've got two options: either you pay, or you pay . . .

OCTAVIO

Why would I pay you, man?

JAROCHO

All right then, are you going to get fresh with me?

OCTAVIO

No, but, come on, why'd you let Pancho loose on him?

JAROCHO

Look: I'll forgive you if you give me your dog.

OCTAVIO

You're fucking crazy.

JAROCHO

Well, you better save up, because I'm going to get my money.

JORGE

If you're so tough, why don't you try charging Ramiro for it? Or what, are you afraid he's going to beat the shit out of you again?

JAROCHO

I'm not afraid . . .

(reveals a pistol butt)

. . . and I'm not going to end up looking like an idiot, you hear me, Octavio?

Octavio pays no attention.

(to his friends)

Let's go.

They pick Pancho up and throw him on the back of the pick-up truck. They leave.

INT. EL CHIVO'S HOUSE — DAY

El Chivo is sitting on a cot in a small room. His five dogs surround him. There is very little furniture: a rickety closet, a bare bulb hanging from the ceiling, a nightstand.

He pulls out the photograph of a bald, fat man in his fifties. He studies it thoroughly. He then removes a 9mm Browning from the desk, hides it in his clothing and leaves the room.

EXT. STREET — DAY

Jorge and Octavio are sitting in an abandoned lot. Octavio has Cofi on a leash. They smoke pot.

                    JORGE
Did you hear el Tamal was caught stealing a car in a supermarket parking lot? They're going to lock him up for four
years. Poor bastard, huh?

                    OCTAVIO
Yep, poor bastard.

He takes a drag.

                    JORGE
Let's see if they don't snag your brother too. The other day
someone told me he held up a drug store.

                    OCTAVIO
No wonder: he even bought himself a sound system.

                    JORGE
Doesn't your mom say anything?

                    OCTAVIO
Man, what's she going to say, he's her favorite. Besides, she
knows the whole deal.

                    JORGE
What about Susana?

OCTAVIO

He doesn't deserve her, man, she's too much of a woman for him.

JORGE

I know, that piece of ass with that asshole . . .

OCTAVIO

Hey, take it easy, he's my brother. And don't talk like that about Susana.

JORGE

All right . . . so what, are you going to finish school?

OCTAVIO

I don't want to, but my mom won't get off my back about it.

JORGE
(pointing at Cofi)
Why don't you put him in a few fights? He might make you some money.

OCTAVIO

No, no way, I don't want to.
(hugs his dog, grabs him by the jowls)
Right, boy?

JORGE

Well, that asshole Jarocho makes a bundle off his dogs.

OCTAVIO

I don't know. I'll see.

Jorge shrugs his shoulders and gives the joint a puff.

INT. DANIEL'S HOUSE – NIGHT

Daniel and Julieta watch TV lying in bed. The phone rings. Daniel picks it up from the nightstand.

DANIEL

Hello . . . Oh, hey! How are you? Good, good . . . no, not much . . .

Julieta grabs the remote and raises the volume.

DANIEL

Hang on a second.

(*to Julieta*)

I can't hear . . .

JULIETA

Neither can I, so leave the room.

She raises the volume even more. Daniel takes the cordless phone and walks into the hall.

DANIEL

What's up? No, I couldn't cancel, but I can make it tomorrow . . . I miss you too . . . OK, don't call and hang up any more, Julieta's starting to suspect . . . No, I'm not mad . . . Yeah, tomorrow at eleven . . .

(*whispering*)

I love you, bye.

He hangs up and returns to the room. Julieta smokes in bed. Daniel goes to the bathroom.

Weren't you going to quit?

JULIETA

Yeah, but I started to get fat.

DANIEL

What you should do is stop eating so much.

Julieta glares at him and blows out more smoke.

JULIETA

That's my problem, isn't it?

DANIEL

Then don't stink up the room.

He dries his hands.

JULIETA

Are you coming to the doctor with me?

19

DANIEL

Damn, I forgot and I've already scheduled an eleven o'clock
meeting.

JULIETA
(*mocking*)

You forgot?

DANIEL

Couldn't you reschedule for the day after tomorrow?

JULIETA

It's the third time I've rescheduled . . .
(*sarcastic*)
. . . so you can come.

DANIEL

Please, change it to the afternoon.

JULIETA

I can never count on you, can I? You only know how to think
about yourself.

She takes a long drag from her cigarette and puts it out.

INT. OCTAVIO'S HOUSE − NIGHT

*Octavio is lying on his bed with his eyes open in the dark. On the other
side of the wall we can hear the panting and thumping of his brother
having sex with Susana.*

INT. OCTAVIO'S HOUSE − DAY

*Octavio is having breakfast. Ramiro arrives in his cashier's uniform
and sits down.*

RAMIRO

What's up with you, man?

OCTAVIO

Nothing.

RAMIRO

Do you have a joint lying around you could give me?

Octavio shakes his head. The mother enters with Ramiro's plate and serves him.

MOTHER

Ramiro . . . I need money.

RAMIRO

I don't have any. They don't pay me till Friday.

MOTHER

And what am I supposed to do? The boy needs diapers and milk. Besides, the eggs you eat don't grow on trees.

RAMIRO

Well, I don't have the money, Mom.

The mother shakes her head and goes back to the kitchen.

OCTAVIO

So, you don't have any money?

RAMIRO

Didn't you hear?

OCTAVIO

All I've heard is that drug stores really pay off.

RAMIRO
(in Octavio's face)
That's my problem and you'd better not say a word.

OCTAVIO

God, you're an idiot.

RAMIRO

Just you squeal on me and I'll crack your face open.

OCTAVIO

Who says being a tough guy makes you any less of an idiot?

EXT. STREET — DAY

El Chivo is discreetly staking out a barbershop. He is without his dogs. Inside is the fifty-year-old man from the photograph. He pays and leaves. His chauffeur waits. The man walks toward the car. He opens the door and starts to get in, when el Chivo pulls out the Browning from his clothes and walks toward him. Their eyes meet fleetingly. El Chivo aims at his head and shoots three times. The man collapses in front of the door. El Chivo runs.

INT. OCTAVIO'S HOUSE — DAY

Octavio is in his room, in front of the closet. He is wearing some pants but is barefoot and shirtless. Susana peers into the half-opened door.

SUSANA
Can I come in?

Octavio grabs a shirt and quickly puts it on. He signals her to come in. She enters.

Going out?

OCTAVIO
Why do you ask?

SUSANA
No reason.

Octavio grabs some socks and shoes and sits on his bed to put them on. Susana stays on her feet, with a worried look on her face. Octavio lifts his head and looks at her.

OCTAVIO
What's up? Is something wrong?

SUSANA
It's just that . . .

She bites her lip; it is difficult for her to speak.

OCTAVIO
What happened?

SUSANA
I've got a problem and I don't know what to do.

Octavio stands up and gets close to her.

OCTAVIO
What's wrong?

22

SUSANA
(*breathes*)

I'm pregnant again.

OCTAVIO

Susana, you just had one and now you're thinking of having another one?

SUSANA

I didn't want to.
(*hangs her head and starts to cry*)
Ramiro is going to kill me.

OCTAVIO

No, come on, he got pissed off the first time and look – he married you.

SUSANA

Yeah, but I don't know if I want to be with him any more.

She cries even more. He doesn't know what to say. She suddenly raises her head.

I can't have the baby, I can't.

OCTAVIO

Are you thinking of having an abortion?

SUSANA
(*desperate*)

What am I supposed to do if I don't have one? What the fuck am I supposed to do?

She starts crying again. He looks at her, pensive.

OCTAVIO

Run away with me.

SUSANA
(*disconcerted*)

What?

OCTAVIO

Yeah, run away with me, let's get out of here.

SUSANA

I'm being serious.

OCTAVIO

So am I.

SUSANA

Don't talk shit, where the hell would we go?

Octavio grabs her by the head and pulls her toward him to kiss her. She pushes him violently.

What the hell are you doing?

OCTAVIO

Run away with me.

She turns around and leaves.

EXT. STREET — NIGHT

Ramiro and el Jaibo, a skinny, gaunt nineteen-year-old with greasy black hair, are inside a run-down Volkswagen Beetle. They watch the movement inside a pharmacy.

RAMIRO

How many are there?

JAIBO

About six women and three men. You ready?

RAMIRO
(*points at a woman*)
Wait and see if the fat lady walks in; I bet she's got money.

They watch the woman walk down the sidewalk. Ramiro pulls out a ski mask and talks as he puts it on.

You ever fucked a fatso like that?

JAIBO

No.

RAMIRO

I have and it's fucking great.

JAIBO

Oh yeah? Who?

RAMIRO

Your mom, man.

JAIBO

Son of a bitch . . .

Ramiro points at a Bital bank on the corner..

RAMIRO

One day we're going to hit that fucking bank, you'll see.

JAIBO

Easy there, superman . . .

RAMIRO

We're going to get into the big leagues, man. I'll just hit that bank
and get the hell out of here; the streets aren't safe any more.

The fat woman walks into the pharmacy. Ramiro adjusts his headgear.

Come on, the fatso's in.

*He opens the door and gets out with the ski mask on, pistol in hand. El
Jaibo does the same. They run toward the pharmacy.*

FADE OUT.

INT. EL CHIVO'S HOUSE – NIGHT

*El Chivo walks into his house followed by his dogs. He has a newspaper
in his hand. He walks into the kitchen and throws it on the table. He
pulls out a pistol and places it next to the newspaper. He pours himself a
glass of milk with a shot of rum.*

He checks the paper. In one of the sections the headlines say, INDUS-
TRIAL ASESINADO *('Prominent Businessman Murdered'). The photograph of the man he killed is printed beside. He picks up a pen and
draws glasses and a mustache on the photograph.*

*When he's done he turns the page and discovers an obituary notice that
says:* 'Norma Sainz, Widow to Esquerra – *El Chivo reads carefully* –
died yesterday at 17:00 hrs./ her daughter María Eugenia, her sis-

ters and bereaved family members painfully announce her passing / the funeral cortège will start tomorrow at 10:30 hrs. at "Los Arcos" cemetery.'

El Chivo raises his hand to his brow; he is in pain. He underlines the time of the cortège and the name of the cemetery. He tears off the page and puts it away.

FADE OUT.

INT. OCTAVIO'S HOUSE – NIGHT

Susana sleeps in her room. Ramiro walks in and suddenly turns on the light. He sits on the bed. She sits up, rubbing her eyes.

SUSANA
What's up, do you want me to make you some dinner?

RAMIRO
No.
(*grabs her by the hand and kisses her*)
Look what I brought you.

He puts some Walkman headphones on her. He presses 'play' and music is heard. She looks at him, amazed.

SUSANA
Thanks . . .

She grabs Ramiro by the shirt and starts to kiss him. He strokes her breasts and she draws close to him.

Lie down . . .

She is about to turn off the light when Ramiro moves away from her. He tickles her ribs and she laughs.

RAMIRO
(*getting up*)
Wait, I brought the kid something too . . .

Susana gets up and takes off the headphones. Ramiro jostles the baby.

SUSANA
Don't wake him up.

26

Why not?

SUSANA

He wasn't feeling well; he only just fell asleep.

Ramiro pays no attention. He picks the baby up and shakes him.

Ramiro, please, don't be a prick.

RAMIRO

He's my son and I know what I'm doing. Hey, kid, hey.

The baby wakes up and, frightened, starts to cry.

SUSANA

He doesn't feel well, dammit!

RAMIRO
(*pointing his finger at her*)

I'm giving you three seconds to shut up. Didn't I just give you a fucking Walkman? You won't stop fucking nagging me even if I'm nice to you.

Susana shuts up. The baby cries. Ramiro pulls out a toy and tries to distract him. One of his hands slips off the baby.

SUSANA
(*alarmed*)

Ramiro, the baby!

RAMIRO

I said, shut up!

He feigns dropping the baby.

God dammit!

Ramiro delicately puts the baby in his cradle and kisses his head.

INT. OCTAVIO'S ROOM – NIGHT

In the next room we see Octavio lying on his bed, listening to what's happening.

FADE OUT.

EXT. ABANDONED LOT — DAY

Octavio and Jorge play a game that involves throwing a switchblade. Cofi watches. Octavio throws the knife.

> JORGE
> Man, she's your brother's woman.

> OCTAVIO
> Yeah, but I liked her way before he did.

> JORGE
> Wake up, man, he beat you to her.

> OCTAVIO
> No way. Besides, Ramiro doesn't care about her.

> JORGE
> But Susana does. It's too risky.

> OCTAVIO
> I can't stop thinking about her.

> JORGE
> There are thousands of women, man. Why do you specifically want to fuck her?

> OCTAVIO
> I don't want to fuck her, I want her to come live with me.

> JORGE
> Oh yeah, and how exactly do you plan to pay the bills?

Octavio points at Cofi.

> You're going to put him in the fights?

Octavio nods.

> And where are you going to get the betting money?

> OCTAVIO
> (*laughs mockingly*)
> I'm going to pimp your sister.

Closes the blade and puts it away.

INT. OCTAVIO'S ROOM — NIGHT

Octavio is lying down in the dark. Panting is heard in the next room again. He seems upset. He suddenly gets up and walks over to his brother's room.

INT. HALLWAY — NIGHT

He knocks furiously on Ramiro and Susana's door.

RAMIRO (O.S.)

Who is it?

OCTAVIO

It's for Susana.

RAMIRO (O.S.)

Who's calling?

OCTAVIO

Her mother.

RAMIRO

Tell her to fuck off.

OCTAVIO

She says it's urgent.

Silence. After a few seconds, Susana walks out in her nightgown. Octavio points at the phone at the end of the hallway. Octavio closes the door and follows her. Susana picks up the receiver and realizes there's no one there. She shows him the phone.

SUSANA

Who called?

OCTAVIO

I did.

SUSANA
(upset)

You're fucking crazy, man.

She heads toward her room. He grabs her by the shoulders from behind and kisses the nape of her neck. She staggers and turns to look at him.

No, Octavio. Not like this . . .

OCTAVIO

Then how?

She shakes her head, walks into her room and closes the door.

EXT. PATIO, MAURICIO'S HOUSE — DAY

Mauricio walks around Cofi. Octavio, Jorge and el Sargento, a tall, dark-skinned man who looks like a bodyguard, watch him. They are in the patio where we saw the first fight.

MAURICIO

This dog doesn't look very good.

JORGE

Well, it killed el Jarocho's dog.

MAURICIO

Do you know how this business works?

OCTAVIO

More or less.

MAURICIO

More or less? Come with me.

EXT. DOG POUND — DAY

They walk round the back of the house and stop at some wire kennels. Inside one is a Rottweiler, in the next one is a pit bull, then a Doberman and in the last one is a Fila. The dogs bark at Cofi, causing a racket.

MAURICIO
(*yelling*)

Sargento, Sargento . . .

El Sargento walks in.

Take this dog over there.

El Sargento takes Cofi away, and the other dogs quiet down.

This is my business. I don't pay taxes, there are no unions or strikes; just clean cash and a few losses every now and then.

(points at the Fila)

This dog has been my best investment. I bought that truck . . .

(points at a 1996 Dodge Ram)

. . . with my earnings. He's old, but he can still fight.

(to Octavio)

We can be partners. You're in with the dog and I'm in with the betting money. We'll go fifty–fifty on the earnings. What do you say?

OCTAVIO

(thinks for a few seconds)

You're on.

MAURICIO

All right, pal, but the deal is for eight fights and we'll see how it goes from there . . .

OCTAVIO

All right.

MAURICIO

But first I want to size your dog up; see him go for a round with Mac here.

OCTAVIO

Sure, but it's going to cost you 5,000 pesos, win or lose.

MAURICIO

(cackles)

Don't bullshit me, man.

OCTAVIO

What if your dog kills mine?

MAURICIO

What if it's the other way around?

OCTAVIO

Maybe, but I haven't bought myself a truck like that yet.

Mauricio laughs heartily. Jorge listens to his friend incredulously.

MAURICIO

I'll give you 2,500, all right?

*Octavio assents. Mauricio takes out the money and pays him. Octavio
counts some bills and gives them to Jorge.*

OCTAVIO

Here, your share.

JORGE
(*puts the money away*)

Cool . . .

MAURICIO

Sargento, bring the dog in . . .

El Sargento returns. He gets the Fila from its kennel.

EXT. PATIO, MAURICIO'S HOUSE — DAY

They bring them into the patio amid the other dogs' barking.

MAURICIO

On three.
(*to Jorge*)

You count.

JORGE

One, two . . .

*Mauricio lets the Fila go on 'two'. Octavio barely has time to get out of
the way when Cofi dodges the Fila's charge, grabs it by the neck and
doesn't let go.*

MAURICIO

That's enough; get your dog.

*Octavio doesn't pay attention. Mauricio motions with his hand for
Sargento to intervene.*

*Sargento grabs Cofi by the collar, shoves a rod in his mouth and pulls
him away. The Fila runs, bleeding, to take refuge in a corner.*

Come round on Saturday at twelve. We'll give Jarocho his
rematch.

Octavio nods.

INT. SUPERMARKET — DAY

Ramiro is at the register, tending to a customer. He gives her her change. Without looking up at the next customer, he checks the barcode on a pack of diapers.

> RAMIRO
> Did you find everything you were looking for?

> OCTAVIO
> My God, the courtesy! Are you trying to be employee of the month?

Ramiro raises his eyes and sees Octavio, who has powdered milk, diapers and bottles in his cart.

> RAMIRO
> What are you doing here?

> OCTAVIO
> Shopping, can't you see?

> RAMIRO
> Where'd you get the money, asshole?

> OCTAVIO
> If you don't have money, I do.

> RAMIRO
> Well, shove it up your ass 'cause I pay for my family's things.

He holds up the diapers.

> OCTAVIO
> Run them up or I'll call the manager.

> RAMIRO
> Son of a bitch!

He grabs Octavio by the neck and pulls him toward him.

> You've got three seconds to get out of here or I'll beat the shit out of you.

OCTAVIO

I'm not Susana, you shit.

He suddenly headbutts him and breaks his nose. Ramiro bleeds and lets him go.

RAMIRO

Son of a bitch . . .

People start to mill around them. Octavio is frightened and runs away.

INT. OCTAVIO'S HOUSE – DAY

Dusk. Susana is playing with the baby in the living room. Octavio comes in with some shopping bags, puts them on the floor and stands next to her.

OCTAVIO

Here . . .

(*he gives her an envelope*)

. . . open it.

Susana takes it and opens it. It is filled with cash.

I'll have more soon.

SUSANA

What for?

OCTAVIO

For us, so you can take care of him . . .

(*points at the baby*)

. . . and him . . .

He points at her stomach.

Susana does not know what to say.

INT. OCTAVIO'S HOUSE – DAY

Octavio is showering. He closes his eyes under the showerhead. Suddenly, through the cloth curtain, he is beaten repeatedly. He falls to the ground. The curtain tears and we see Ramiro striking him with a billy-club. Octavio tries to defend himself, but Ramiro will not stop. Octavio's head is bleeding.

RAMIRO

Stay the hell out of my business, you little shit.

Octavio lies bleeding as water hits his face.

FADE OUT.

EXT. CEMETERY — DAY

El Chivo is sitting on an old Valiant. In the distance, he sees a group of people paying their last respects. It is a modern cemetery. He specifically watches a young woman, about twenty-two years old, dressed in black, who seems inconsolable. Next to her, a woman in her fifties with dyed blonde hair, slightly overweight, comforts her.

They finish lowering the coffin into the grave. The girl cries. El Chivo gets off the car. The mourners start to walk toward their cars. The fifty-year-old woman spots el Chivo and walks toward him.

WOMAN

What are you doing here?

CHIVO

Having a stroll.

WOMAN

Well, go stroll somewhere else. Don't bother us . . .
(*pointing at the girl*)
. . . and least of all her.

CHIVO

What I do or don't do is my problem.

WOMAN

You're dead to her. Don't forget that.

She walks away angrily. El Chivo watches the girl get into a car.

INT. MAURICIO'S HOUSE — DAY

JAROCHO
(*to Mauricio*)

What's up, Porky?

MAURICIO

Just hanging around, Jarocho.

El Jarocho doesn't greet Jorge or Octavio.

JAROCHO
(*to Mauricio*)
Since when do you let girls fight?

MAURICIO

Since they have good dogs.

JAROCHO

If he's that good, why don't you put down fifteen?

OCTAVIO

He's better than any of your dogs.

JAROCHO

I'm talking to the ringmaster, Princess. So what, fatman, fifteen?

MAURICIO

Make it ten.

JAROCHO

All right then.

They move into the arena. Jarocho moves into one corner, Octavio to the other.

MAURICIO

Place your bets.

The bookies start collecting bets. Mauricio stands in the middle of the ring. There is a constant murmur. The bookies signal Mauricio that they've finished.

Psych 'em.

Jarocho and Octavio take the muzzles off their dogs. Octavio bends down, grabs Cofi by the head and pets him.

OCTAVIO

Tear his throat out, boy.

MAURICIO
MAURICIO

Ready?

The dogs are pulled into the corners.

Go.

The dogs run at each other.

FADE OUT.

EXT. SUSANA'S MOTHER'S HOUSE — DAY

Susana arrives at a run-down apartment building. She carries the baby with her. She pushes the front door open and walks up some stairs.

INT. SUSANA'S MOTHER'S APARTMENT — DAY

Susana opens the door to apartment 203. The metal '3' is missing. She walks in.

SUSANA

Hi, Mom.

She closes the door.

SUSANA'S MOTHER

I'm over here.

Susana heads to the kitchen. Her mother, a fortysomething, thin, wrinkled woman with a ridiculous hairdo and bad makeup is sitting at the kitchen table, smoking.

Hey, sweetie. Oh good, you brought me the baby.

The mother takes the baby and sits him on her lap. Although she is not incoherent, she seems nervous and moves brusquely.

SUSANA

How are you?

SUSANA'S MOTHER

Fine, sweetie.

The mother grows quiet, slightly lost. She suddenly smiles and shakes a matchbox to amuse the baby.

He really is cute. He looks more and more like your grandpa Nacho.

The baby tries to grab the matches; his grandmother quickly hides them.

Honey, do you have a cigarette? This is my last one.

SUSANA
No, Mom, I haven't smoked since Rodrigo was born.

SUSANA'S MOTHER
You're right, it's bad for you. I'd better put this one out; I don't want to harm the baby.

She puts the cigarette out in an ashtray and is silent again. Susana plays with her baby.

Listen, sweetie, do you have some money I could borrow . . .?

SUSANA
What for?

SUSANA'S MOTHER
You know, for women's things . . .

SUSANA
Tell me what they are and I'll get them for you.

SUSANA'S MOTHER
I'd rather you left me the money.

She seems anxious. Susana pulls out a fifty-peso bill and leaves it on the table.

Thanks, but do you have a little more?

Susana shakes her head.

Oh, it doesn't matter, thanks anyway.

She smiles a stupid smile.

INT. MAURICIO'S HOUSE – DAY

Octavio pets Cofi, who is bleeding from one of his ears. Standing next to him are Mauricio and Jorge. El Jarocho walks up to Mauricio.

Behind him are Javier, el Chispas and Alvaro, who is dragging a dead Rottweiler.

> JAROCHO
> (*to Mauricio, angry*)

You were lucky.

> MAURICIO

You had to lose some day.

El Jarocho raises his eyebrows and points his index finger at Octavio.

> JAROCHO

That's two you owe me, Princess.

He leaves. His three friends follow, dragging the Rottweiler. The body leaves a line of blood.

INT. OCTAVIO'S HOUSE – DAY

Octavio enters. He walks up the stairs in twos and goes into Ramiro's room. He finds Susana asleep in bed beside the baby. Octavio taps her shoulder and she wakes up, startled.

> SUSANA

What happened?

> OCTAVIO

Here.

He gives her some bills. Susana sits up and takes them.

They're ours, just don't keep them there . . .
> (*points at the nightstand*)

. . . my brother might steal them. Do you have another place to put them?

> SUSANA
> (*sleepy*)

The other day I hid the cash in a shoebox inside the closet.

Octavio opens the closet. There are boxes piled on each other. Susana points one out.

That one.

Octavio grabs a blue box. He puts the rest of the money in there as well.

OCTAVIO
This box will be like our bank, OK? Just yours and mine.

SUSANA
Octavio, are you stealing too?

OCTAVIO
No, I swear this is good money, Susana, so you can go away with me.

SUSANA
Go away with you? Can't you see?

OCTAVIO
You're the one that can't see. Look: Jorge has some cousins in Ciudad Juárez. He told me we can stay with them. We'll run a store or something. We've got money, it'll be fine.

SUSANA
I don't want any more problems. Don't you get it?

Octavio is quiet for a moment.

Don't you get it?

OCTAVIO
Run away with me . . .

Susana looks in his eyes, caresses his cheek and shakes her head.

INT. MAURICIO'S HOUSE – DAY

Octavio is in the arena with Cofi and another dogfighter in the other corner. An eight-year-old boy and a seven-year-old girl stare at the dogs in awe while their father gets drunk.

INT. MAURICIO'S HOUSE – DAY

Mauricio is giving Octavio some money. Octavio counts some out and gives it to Jorge.

INT. OCTAVIO'S HOUSE – NIGHT

Octavio places rows of bills on his bed.

INT. 7-11 STORE – NIGHT

Ramiro and Jaibo hold up a 7-11.

INT. OCTAVIO'S HOUSE – DAY

Octavio, Ramiro, their mother, Susana and the baby have breakfast in silence.

INT. OCTAVIO'S HOUSE – NIGHT

Octavio gives Susana a wad of cash. She puts it in the blue shoebox.

INT. SUPERMARKET BATHROOM – DAY

Ramiro has sex with his neighboring check-out girl, both in uniform.

INT. MAURICIO'S HOUSE – DAY

Octavio collects money from Mauricio. Cofi is at his side. A dog lies inert on the arena. Jarocho looks at him spitefully.

INT. MAURICIO'S HOUSE – DAY

Jarocho and Mauricio are sitting at a table. They are talking. Jarocho is explaining something and Mauricio listens attentively.

    FADE OUT.

INT. OCTAVIO'S HOUSE – DAY

Octavio watches TV in his room. Cofi lies next to him. Ramiro walks into the room.

                OCTAVIO
I didn't give you permission to come in.

Ramiro sits on the bed. He puts a pillow behind his head.

                RAMIRO
What are you watching?

OCTAVIO

What do you care?

RAMIRO
(*cynical*)
Change the channel. I don't like this show.

OCTAVIO

What do you want?

RAMIRO

Someone told me you're getting rich off my dog.

OCTAVIO

Your dog? This is my dog.

RAMIRO

Oh, man, you really are full of shit. This dog is as much mine
as it is yours and that makes half of what you make mine.
Besides, look at how you're treating him.
(*shows him one of Cofi's ears*)
It looks like you don't care that much about your beloved
dog.

OCTAVIO

I care more about him than you can imagine, and if it's
money you're after I'm not going to give you one peso.

Ramiro pulls out a gun and holds it to Cofi's head. Cofi wags his tail.

RAMIRO

It's real simple: if you don't give me a cut of the profits, I'll
blow your piggy bank's brains out.

*He pulls the trigger, but the gun isn't loaded. Octavio jumps when he
hears the 'click'.*

Next time I will kill him. So you'd better start getting my
money.

Ramiro gets up, smiles, puts the gun away and struts out.

EXT. STREET — DAY

El Chivo stakes out the girl's house. She walks out and heads for her car. He moves near her. Their eyes meet. She looks at him fearfully and hurries into her car. He watches her go.

INT. OCTAVIO'S HOUSE – DAY

Susana and the baby play on the floor. Octavio walks in and sits next to them. He cuddles the baby.

OCTAVIO

Hey, kid, what's going on?

The baby laughs. Octavio puts his head on the baby's belly and makes him laugh even more. Susana watches them, amused. When he's done, Octavio pulls out a wad of cash. Susana bites her lip.

SUSANA

You've given me a lot; it's enough to live on for two years.

OCTAVIO

Live them with me.

Susana looks at him tenderly.

SUSANA

Why, Octavio?

OCTAVIO

Why what?

SUSANA

Why do you want to live with me?

OCTAVIO

Don't you know yet?

SUSANA

Yes, I do.

OCTAVIO

Come here.

She moves toward him, and he kisses her on the mouth. They start to make out. The baby crawls around them, thoroughly amused. They get naked and start to make love on the floor.

INT. DANIEL'S HOUSE — NIGHT

Daniel walks into his daughters' room in the dark. He looks at them asleep in their beds. He caresses their cheeks and looks at them both with some sadness in his eyes. He tucks them in and walks out.

INT. MAURICIO'S HOUSE — DAY

Mauricio, Octavio and Jorge are sitting at a table. Mauricio is having breakfast.

> MAURICIO
> *(to Octavio)*
> You sure you don't want any?

> OCTAVIO
> No, thanks.

> MAURICIO
> What about you, Georgie boy?

> JORGE
> Yeah, I'll have some beans.

El Champiñon serves Jorge, and he starts to eat heartily.

> MAURICIO
> I've got a deal for you. El Jarocho says he's got a real vicious dog and wants to pit him against Cofi.

> JORGE
> Cofi'll shred him.

> MAURICIO
> He wants to bet forty.

> OCTAVIO
> *(pensive)*
> Forty? Are we going to go for it?

> MAURICIO
> Not me. That's too much money for me. If you want in, you're in alone.

OCTAVIO

What about our deal?

MAURICIO

We said eight fights and we've done fifteen. This is as far as I go. You made your money and I made mine, OK?

OCTAVIO

All right. When does he want to fight?

Mauricio starts licking his plate while he talks.

MAURICIO

This Saturday. He wants a fight at the Trujillos' place; no outside bets, just you and him.

OCTAVIO

All right.

Mauricio finishes lapping up his plate and gives it to el Champiñon, who returns it directly to the shelf. Jorge looks at his plate in disgust.

MAURICIO

Shall I set it up?

Octavio nods.

OCTAVIO

Hey, Mauricio, I need you to help me out with something.

INT. OCTAVIO'S HOUSE — NIGHT

Octavio and Susana are showering together. They kiss and start having sex under the water.

INT. SUPERMARKET — NIGHT

Ramiro rings up products at the register.

EXT. SUPERMARKET — NIGHT

An old Dodge Dart parks in front of the supermarket. El Sargento, Mauricio and three other men who look like bodyguards get out of the car.

INT. OCTAVIO'S HOUSE — NIGHT

Octavio and Susana are still having sex.

INT. SUPERMARKET — NIGHT

Ramiro is saying goodbye to the same check-out girl from before. He kisses her on the lips and feels her up. She laughs.

EXT. SUPERMARKET — NIGHT

Two of the bodyguards stand by the supermarket exit.

INT. OCTAVIO'S HOUSE — NIGHT

Octavio gropes Susana's breasts.

EXT. SUPERMARKET — NIGHT

Ramiro walks out, absent-minded. Far off, Mauricio signals the bodyguards. They walk up behind him and, with el Sargento's help, they shove him into the Dart. Mauricio walks away.

EXT. ABANDONED LOT — NIGHT

They push Ramiro out into the lot. They throw him to the ground and start to kick him savagely. Ramiro writhes.

INT. OCTAVIO'S HOUSE — NIGHT

Octavio and Susana orgasm in the shower.

INT. OCTAVIO'S ROOM — NIGHT

Susana and Octavio get dressed. He kisses her belly.

> OCTAVIO
> How's the baby doing?

> SUSANA
> Growing, I guess.

> OCTAVIO
> What are you going to call it?

SUSANA

If it's a girl . . . Susana, and if . . .

OCTAVIO

If it's a boy Octavio, right?

She just smiles.

I've got everything ready so that we can leave on Sunday, but
I'm going to need some money from the box: I'm going for
the big one on Saturday.

SUSANA
(*hugging Cofi*)

Don't make him fight any more; we've got enough.

Octavio grabs the dog by the jowls.

OCTAVIO

This is the last one, boy, I promise.
(*turns to Susana*)
What time did you buy the tickets to Ciudad Juárez for?

SUSANA

The bus leaves at twelve. Ramiro'll still be working.

OCTAVIO

Don't worry about Ramiro. He's never going to mess with us
again, you'll see.

Susana looks at him strangely.

Are you afraid?

SUSANA

It's tough . . .

OCTAVIO

Are you afraid?

She looks at him without answering.

INT. SUSANA'S MOTHER'S HOUSE — DAY

Susana walks up the stairs and opens the door. She is in her uniform.

47

SUSANA

Mom, Mom . . .

She looks in the kitchen and living room and cannot find her. Everything is a mess. She finds her in her room, with a glass in her hand, completely drunk.

SUSANA'S MOTHER

Sweetie, you're home . . .

SUSANA
(*upset*)

Where's the baby?

SUSANA'S MOTHER

The baby?
(*raises her eyebrows*)
The baby is . . . The baby?

SUSANA

Yes, Mom, the baby.

Susana's mother doesn't answer. Susana looks for him. She finds him in the other room, dirty and soiled. She can see he's exhausted from crying so much. Susana is about to say something to her mother, but decides against it and leaves.

INT. OCTAVIO'S HOUSE – NIGHT

Octavio comes in, goes into the kitchen and opens the refrigerator. He is rummaging for food when his mother walks in.

OCTAVIO

Hey, Mom.

The mother leans on the sink, serious.

MOTHER

Haven't you heard what happened to your brother today?

OCTAVIO

Nope.

MOTHER

You haven't? Well, he came in all beat up.

OCTAVIO
(*mocking*)
Some happy shopper must have gotten angry.

He serves himself some milk. His mother looks at him fixedly.

MOTHER
Your brother received a death threat . . .

OCTAVIO
God knows what he's up to.

The mother keeps her serious gaze on Octavio.

MOTHER
He left the house with Susana and the baby today . . .

OCTAVIO
(*surprised*)

Where did he go?

MOTHER
I don't know, and I don't know if they're coming back.

OCTAVIO

What?

Octavio looks at her, totally distraught. He runs up to Ramiro's room and opens the closet: nothing. The blue box is on the floor, empty. Octavio picks it up and checks it: nothing. He throws it away furiously and punches the wall repeatedly.

His mother watches him in disapproval from the door frame.

INT. SUSANA'S MOTHER'S APARTMENT – DAY

Octavio knocks on the door desperately. Susana's mother opens it, extremely drunk. He barges in and starts looking for her. Susana's mother can barely stand up.

OCTAVIO

Where's Susana?

She shrugs her shoulders. Octavio faces her.

Where is she?

49

She doesn't answer and collapses on to the couch. She closes her eyes. Octavio walks out furiously.

INT. OCTAVIO'S HOUSE – DAY

Full-screen shot of a TV host.

> HOST
> Today on our show we've got a surprise no man will want to miss.

The TV camera pulls back and shows him next to a hostess.

> I would like to welcome one of the most beautiful women in Latin America: Valeria Amaya.

Valeria walks in. She is wearing a miniskirt that shows her magnificent legs. She is stunning. The host stands up and kisses her hello. Valeria sits down and crosses her legs. The camera pulls back and reveals Jorge and Octavio counting money in the room.

> OCTAVIO
> (*pensive*)
> I've got to find her, man.

> JORGE
> Man, I told you, she pulled a fast one.

> OCTAVIO
> It wasn't her. I'm sure it was Ramiro.

They become silent and go back to counting money.

> HOST
> Valeria, it is a pleasure to have you with us.

> VALERIA
> The pleasure is all mine.

> HOST
> This has been your breakout year, hasn't it? You're the image for Enchant in Latin America, something many models wish they could be.

Valeria smiles. Octavio stops counting money.

OCTAVIO

I swear I'm going to find her, man. How much do you have?

JORGE

Ten. What about you?

OCTAVIO

Eleven. Let's see if el Jarocho will go for it.

JORGE

I've got about 3,000 at home I can lend you.

Octavio assents and starts putting the money in his jacket pocket. Jorge watches TV.

Man, is she hot.

HOSTESS

And, if I may be indiscreet: I've heard rumors that you've got a new boyfriend.

VALERIA

They aren't rumors: it's the truth.

HOSTESS

Is that so?

VALERIA

Of course, and I even invited him to the show. Honey, come here . . .

A tall, handsome man walks in.

HOST

Well, look at that! It's none other than Andrés Salgado!

They hug. Andrés kisses the hostess hello and sits next to Valeria. He takes her by the hand.

HOSTESS

You really are lucky, Andrés. Let's give them a hand.

Andrés and Valeria smile. They kiss. The audience claps. Octavio finishes putting the money away.

OCTAVIO

Let's go.

They leave without turning off the TV. The camera slowly dollies in toward the screen.

HOSTESS

And, just to push my luck a little more, do you plan on getting married?

VALERIA

Not at the moment, but we already have a son.

HOST

A son?

VALERIA

Sure, look . . .

(*claps*)

Richi, come here, baby.

A white, miniature French poodle runs onscreen and jumps on to her lap. The audience claps again.

This is my baby.

HOST

Well, he certainly takes after Andrés . . .

Everyone laughs.

EXT. STREET – DAY

Octavio, Jorge and Cofi arrive in the gray Rabbit and park in front of the Trujillos' house. El Sargento opens their door.

INT. TRUJILLO HOUSE – DAY

They enter. It is a large house with a huge garden where there is an empty, abandoned pool. The place exudes decadence. There are very few people. Jarocho is waiting for them with a huge Fila.

JAROCHO

I thought you'd chickened out.

52

OCTAVIO

Well, I didn't.

MAURICIO

Have you got the 40,000?

Octavio pulls out the wad of cash and hands it over.

OCTAVIO

I could only get twenty-five.

Mauricio looks at Octavio and then at Jarocho.

MAURICIO
(*to Jarocho*)

Is twenty-five OK?

JAROCHO

All right, let's go.

They go to their corners.

MAURICIO

Psych 'em.

They take the muzzles off and rile the dogs up. The Fila is ferocious.

Let them go.

The dogs run at each other. Cofi quickly gets the upper hand. He grabs the Fila by the neck and clenches. He is clearly in control.

Suddenly a shot is heard and Cofi collapses, wounded. Both dogs are inert: one from the gunshot, the other from the fight. Octavio stares stupefied at el Jarocho, who holds a gun in his hand.

OCTAVIO

What the fuck are you doing, man?

JAROCHO

Fight's over, isn't it?

OCTAVIO

My dog was winning, you asshole, why'd you shoot him?

JAROCHO

My finger slipped, Princess, what do you want me to do about it?

OCTAVIO
(*to Mauricio*)

What is this shit?

MAURICIO

Don't get me into this; this is your problem.
(*pulls out the money*)
Here's your money . . .
(*gives it to Jarocho*)
. . . and here's yours.

He gives it to Octavio, who, astounded, receives it mechanically.

JORGE

Mauricio, this isn't fair.

MAURICIO

You sort it out, keep me out of this.

JAROCHO

Stop whining, girls; that's the way this business works. And you'd better get the fuck out of here; we don't want things to heat up any more than they already are.

Jarocho holds up the gun he just shot. Alvaro and Javier open their jackets and show more weapons.

(*mocking*)
And if you want to go squeal to Ramiro, you tell him I'll wait for him right here.

Octavio and Jorge, defeated, decide to get Cofi out. Octavio puts the money in his jacket, puts his hands under his dog and, together with Jorge, carries him into the Rabbit.

EXT. STREET — DAY

They struggle to put Cofi into the back seat. Octavio starts the car and leaves it on. He gets out.

JORGE

What are you going to do?

OCTAVIO

Keep it running and leave the door open.

Octavio walks into the house again.

INT. TRUJILLO HOUSE — DAY

He walks resolutely through the halls. As he does so, he takes out his switchblade and opens it. He arrives where el Jarocho is talking to Mauricio.

JAROCHO

Forget something, Princess?

Octavio does not answer and, with one swift motion, stabs el Jarocho twice and runs out. The others are slow to react. While el Jarocho collapses, Alvaro and Javier jump behind him.

ALVARO

Get him, get him . . .

EXT. STREET — DAY

Octavio reaches the street and jumps in the Rabbit. They take off at full speed. Alvaro, Javier and el Chispas run out as well. They force a man to leave his white Topaz at gunpoint and the initial chase begins again.

FADE OUT.

TITLE OVER BLACK: 'WHITE DOG'

INT. TV STUDIO — DAY

We see an image of Valeria, Andrés and the host on a TV monitor.

HOST

We would like to thank Valeria Amaya and Andrés Salgado for coming on the show.

The camera pulls back, and we see they are in a television studio.

Don't go away. We'll be right back with more after this.

Everyone holds a smile on camera. They cut to a commercial break. Valeria and Andrés stand up and take their microphones off. The hostess walks up to them while the host has his makeup touched up.

> HOSTESS
> *(to Valeria)*
> I thought you were seeing someone else. There were lots of rumors.

> VALERIA
> Well, there you go . . . People are so gossipy.

The floor manager calls the hostess.

> FLOOR MANAGER
> Laura, get to your spot, twenty seconds people, nineteen . . .

The hostess returns to her spot. Valeria blows a kiss to the host, waves goodbye to the hostess and walks out holding Andrés' hand.

INT. TV STATION HALLWAY – DAY

Andrés and Valeria walk down the hall.

> ANDRÉS
> What are you going to do today?

> VALERIA
> I don't know, why?

> ANDRÉS
> Let me take you to lunch.

They walk out into the parking lot.

EXT. TV STATION PARKING LOT – DAY

> VALERIA
> I don't think I can go. Thanks anyway.

> ANDRÉS
> Are you going to tell me, Andrés Salgado, that you can't go?

Valeria walks toward her car: a gold Honda Accord. She opens the door and puts Richi in.

VALERIA

Look, Andrés, one thing is one thing . . .

ANDRÉS

. . . and another thing's another, I know, but it's a surprise
you're going to love.

VALERIA

(*thinks*)

All right.

EXT. STREET – DAY

They park near the restaurants and get out. She is holding Richi.

VALERIA

What restaurant are we going to?

ANDRÉS

I didn't say we were going to a restaurant . . .

(*mischievous*)

. . . I said I would take you to lunch.

*He takes her by the arm and walks her into an apartment building
characteristic of the 'Condesa' neighborhood. He opens the glass door.*

INT. APARTMENT – DAY

*They enter a nice apartment, furnished austerely. Two places are ele-
gantly set up in a small dining room. Valeria stops in front of a sofa.*

VALERIA

This sofa is just like the one I have at my place.

ANDRÉS

It's not like it: it is it. And if you walk into the bedroom you'll
find your clothes, perfumes . . .

VALERIA

(*irritated*)

What's your fucking problem?

Andrés walks toward a window and opens it.

ANDRÉS

That's not all: look at the view.

Valeria looks out. Two buildings down is the billboard with her image on it.

VALERIA

You're scaring me.

Andrés sticks his hand in his pocket and pulls out a key.

ANDRÉS

Here, this is the key to your apartment.

VALERIA

My apartment?

DANIEL (O.S.)

Yeah, your apartment, our apartment.

Valeria turns around and sees Daniel. She runs toward him and, midway, falls into a hole that cracks open in the wooden floor.

DANIEL

Watch out!

Daniel hugs her and helps her out.

VALERIA

Oh, darling, darling, darling . . .

They kiss passionately before Andrés' condescending stare. Valeria tries to walk and limps.

What's up with the hole?

DANIEL

I had enough to pay for the apartment, not to fix it up.

VALERIA
(*kissing him*)

It doesn't matter . . .

ANDRÉS

All right, lovey doves, my work here is done.

Valeria hugs him.

VALERIA
(*excited*)

Thank you so much . . .

She kisses him on the cheek.

ANDRÉS

See you later, gorgeous.

He walks toward the door. Daniel walks with him.

DANIEL

Thanks for the help.

ANDRÉS

Thanks for the magazine cover.

They shake hands. Andrés leaves and Daniel goes back in. Valeria is looking at a painting on the wall.

VALERIA

An Ehremberg. Where did you get it?

Daniel looks at her and sighs.

DANIEL

I spoke with Julieta.

VALERIA
(*surprised*)

You did?

Daniel nods.

And?

DANIEL

As of today, we're separated.

VALERIA

Today, as in . . . today?

Daniel nods.

You'd better not be lying to me, because I'll die.

DANIEL

As of tonight I'm sleeping here with you.

VALERIA

Are you sure about this?

DANIEL

I am; have you chickened out?

VALERIA

No, sweetie, no, I just can't believe it.

Valeria kisses him repeatedly. She suddenly pulls away and looks at him seriously.

What about the girls? They'll be hurt, won't they?

DANIEL
(*sadly*)

It'll hurt me even more, but they'll have to accept it and get used to it. They're not the first girls this has happened to.

Valeria strokes his face. Daniel pulls away from her and points at the kitchen.

The food's going to burn: I left it on a low flame.

VALERIA

What's for lunch?

DANIEL

Minestrone, baby palm salad, almond trout and mango for dessert.
(*goes to the dining room and pulls out a chair*)
Madame.

Valeria sits down. Daniel walks into the kitchen. Valeria picks up one of the fine-cut crystal wine glasses.

VALERIA

Daniel, what are toasting with?

Silence. Then Daniel walks out.

DANIEL

Shit! The wine . . . I knew I forgot something. I won't be long.

(*starts taking off his apron*)
Would you keep an eye on the trout in the meantime?

VALERIA

No, honey, you know I'm capable of burning scrambled eggs.
Better let me go get the wine.

DANIEL

Nonsense, you're my guest.

VALERIA

Guest, in my own house?

*Daniel doesn't answer back. Valeria grabs her bag, picks Richi up and
gives Daniel a long kiss.*

I'll be back soon.

She leaves.

INT. VALERIA'S CAR — DAY

*Valeria drives looking for a wine shop. Richi runs to the window every
now and then to bark at something.*

*They reach a stoplight. She stops and pulls Richi back. He is barking
at el Chivo and his five dogs.*

VALERIA

Shh, Richi . . .

*The light turns green. Valeria accelerates when suddenly a silver Rabbit
drives into the intersection at full speed. They crash violently. Valeria's
car has its side destroyed. The car stops at the avenue divider.*

FADE OUT.

INT. HOSPITAL — NIGHT

*Daniel and Andrés are sitting in a waiting room, a fat woman in front
of them. Daniel, demolished, rests his head on his left hand. Andrés
stares into space. The woman scrutinizes Andrés.*

LADY

Excuse me.

Andrés doesn't pay attention.

Excuse me.

Andrés turns around.

Aren't you Andrés Salgado, the movie star?

ANDRÉS
No, ma'am.

He stares off into space again. The woman looks at a magazine and, restless, looks at him again.

LADY
I'm sure you're Andrés Salgado. Don't lie to me.

ANDRÉS
No, I'm not.

LADY
I don't believe you.

Daniel sits up and, furious, faces her.

DANIEL
Didn't you hear him? He is not Andrés Salgado, h-e i-s n-o-t
A-n-d-r-é-s S-a-l-g-a-d-o.

LADY
Take it easy.

DANIEL
Then stop fucking bothering us.

LADY
How rude!

She gets up and walks into the next waiting room. Daniel sits back down.

FADE OUT.

INT. HOSPITAL — NIGHT

Daniel and Andrés are sitting in the waiting room staring at the floor.

A photographer stealthily takes a photograph of them. Andrés sees him and throws an ashtray at him.

INT. HOSPITAL — NIGHT

Daniel and Andrés are still in the waiting room. A doctor appears, dressed in surgical clothes. He sits next to Daniel. It is obvious that they know each other. The doctor sees a pack of cigarettes on the table.

                    DOCTOR
Can I have one?

Daniel nods. The doctor lights the cigarette and exhales. It is obvious that he's looking for the right words.

                    DANIEL
How is she?

                    DOCTOR
It's hard to say at this point. She was in shock from the hemorrhage, she had a double fracture in her tibia and an exposed fractured femur. Her femoral biceps was almost entirely severed. It's a miracle she's alive.

                    DANIEL
But she's going to be OK?

                    DOCTOR
I believe so.

                    DANIEL
When can I see her?

                    DOCTOR
I don't know, probably the day after tomorrow. It depends on how quickly she recovers.

The doctor gives the cigarette another puff. He looks exhausted.

Does she have any family we should notify?

                    DANIEL
Her family lives in Spain and . . . I don't think I can get in touch with them.

DOCTOR

Do you take responsibility?

Daniel nods. The doctor puts the cigarette out and stands up. Daniel and Andrés get up as well.

DANIEL

Thanks, Ignacio.

DOCTOR

No problem.

They shake hands.

See you. Give my regards to Julieta.
                    (*notices his mistake*)
Sorry – habit. Give my love to your daughters.

DANIEL

Don't worry about it . . .

They pat each other on the back. He says goodbye to Andrés.

DOCTOR

Good night.

Leaves.

FADE OUT.

INT. HOSPITAL ROOM – DAY

Daniel is in a hospital room, reading on a couch. A nurse walks in pulling a bed on wheels while another nurse pushes. Valeria is connected to various IVs. Her left leg is bandaged from hip to toe. Daniel sits up. The nurses set the bed up.

NURSE

(*to Daniel, in a low voice*)
Don't talk to her too much: you'll tire her.

Daniel nears the bed. He grabs Valeria by the hand.

DANIEL

Honey . . .

64

His voice chokes up. Valeria opens and closes her eyes. The nurses walk out.

                    VALERIA
I won't be able to play football any more.

Both smile. She groans in doing so.

                    DANIEL
Shhh, relax.

                    VALERIA
How's Richi?

                    DANIEL
He's fine. At home – our home.

                    VALERIA
Our home.

She closes her eyes and opens them again.

Don't tell my father about this . . .

                    DANIEL
It's about time you two spoke, don't you think?

                    VALERIA
I don't want to. Besides, he might even say I deserve it.
Please, don't tell him.

Her face shows profound concern, even while sedated.

                    DANIEL
Sure, honey, sure.

FADE OUT.

INT. HOSPITAL ROOM – NIGHT

Daniel is on the couch, covered with a blanket. Valeria has her eyes open.

                    VALERIA
Daniel, are you awake?

DANIEL

What's up?

He sits up.

VALERIA

Daniel . . . I'm scared . . .

He stands next to her and grabs her hand.

DANIEL

You've been very brave.

VALERIA

The truth is that I'm scared to death.

She starts crying. Daniel hugs her.

DANIEL

Everything is going to be fine, honey, you'll see.

FADE OUT.

INT. APARTMENT – DAY

The door opens. Daniel wheels Valeria into the apartment. Richi barks and jumps on to her lap.

VALERIA

Richi, Richi, my baby . . .

Richi licks her. Valeria still has her arm and leg bandaged. Daniel wheels her into the dining room. It is still set up the way it was before the accident. Her eyes light up.

DANIEL

One more time, the menu: minestrone soup, baby palm salad, almond trout and mangos for desert. And to toast: a Château Lafique '65.

Valeria holds him with her right arm. Her eyes moisten.

VALERIA

Thank you, love, really, from the bottom of my heart.

66

INT. ROOM — NIGHT

Daniel helps Valeria from the wheelchair into bed. Valeria is lying down. Daniel starts stroking her breasts.

> VALERIA
> *(laughing)*

What are you doing?

> DANIEL

Giving you a check-up.

He unbuttons her blouse and starts kissing her breasts.

INT. APARTMENT — NIGHT

Both sleep. Valeria wakes Daniel.

> VALERIA

Daniel . . . Daniel . . .

> DANIEL

Mmmhhhh . . .

> VALERIA

I need to go to the bathroom. I've needed to go for the last hour.

> DANIEL

Coming.

He walks around the bed, sticks his hands under her, and carries her toward the bathroom.

> VALERIA

Daniel, are you crazy?

He barely manages to get her in. When he tries to sit her on the toilet, Daniel slips and she falls on top of him. Nothing serious happens and they both laugh. He puts her on the toilet again.

Can you help me?

> DANIEL

Do what?

VALERIA

Take my panties off.

He takes them off. She starts to urinate while he kisses her.

FADE OUT.

INT. APARTMENT — DAY

Daniel is dressed. Valeria practices using her wheelchair in the living room.

DANIEL

Are you sure you'll be OK?

VALERIA

Look, I'm an expert.

She turns right, left, moves back and forward.

DANIEL

What if you need something?

VALERIA

I've got Richi.

Daniel looks at her, worried.

Go on, I'll be fine.

Daniel gives her a kiss.

DANIEL

The lady I told you about is coming in tomorrow morning . . .

VALERIA

I don't want a maid. I don't like people serving me.

DANIEL

She won't bother you; just in and out, OK?

Valeria looks at him unconvinced

OK?

She agrees reluctantly. Daniel gives her another kiss.

Don't even think of trying to walk.

VALERIA

What if there's an earthquake?

DANIEL

Let the building collapse. Do not get out of your chair.
(*kisses her again*)
I'll be back at eight at the latest.

Daniel leaves, and Valeria blows him a kiss. She is lost in thought in the living room. She sees the billboard through the window.

INT. ROOM — DAY

Valeria watches TV. She flips through all the channels in frustration.

INT. LIVING ROOM — DAY

Valeria cuts Richi's nails with him on her lap.

INT. LIVING ROOM — DAY

Valeria listens to music on a Walkman and spins around in her chair.

INT. ROOM — DAY

Valeria plays solitaire on the dining-room table. The phone rings. She barely picks it up in time.

VALERIA

Hello . . . hello . . .

No one answers. She hangs up.

EXT. STREET — DAY

El Chivo watches the young woman's house. She walks out and gets into a red Cavalier. She drives off. El Chivo makes sure no one sees him and opens the door with a picklock. He walks in and closes the door behind him.

INT. HOUSE — DAY

It is a medium-sized house: living room, dining room and three upstairs bedrooms. It is furnished rustically, in good taste. The couches are made of wool. Some original paintings and posters from Miró and Klee exhibitions hang on the wall.

There are also some family pictures: the young woman when she was a girl; the young woman between a blonde woman like the one at the cemetery and a slender man in his fifties with glasses; a professional degree with a photograph of the man that says: 'Ricardo Esquerra García, Architect'.

Some art and architecture magazines are on the living-room table. El Chivo goes up the stairs and walks into the young woman's room. The bed is unmade. He sits on the mattress and touches the sheets. He checks the photographs on the nightstand. In one of them she is standing next to the blonde woman. He puts it back.

He walks into the bathroom. There are some panties hanging on the shower's sliding door. El Chivo picks them up and stretches them. He puts them back and goes back into the room. He pulls the photograph out of its frame, puts it in his worn jacket and leaves.

FADE OUT.

INT. LIVING ROOM – DAY

Valeria is in the living room with Richi. She throws a rubber ball at him which he fetches and brings back. She does it a number of times. On one throw, the ball bounces into the hole where Valeria had fallen. The dog runs after the ball and falls in the hole. It takes him a while to get out.

VALERIA
Richi, Richi . . . here, boy.

Richi does not come out. Valeria wheels herself to the edge of the hole.

Richi, Richi.

She whistles.

Dog bark echoes are heard. Valeria lowers herself on to the floor with difficulty and looks into the hole. It connects to the entire floor. There are about 20 cm between the wood and the concrete under it.

> (*clapping her hands*)
Richi, sweetie, here . . .

We hear distant barking. The dog does not come out.

FADE OUT.

INT. APARTMENT — NIGHT

Daniel gets home and opens the door.

> DANIEL
I'm home.

No answer. He finds Valeria sitting in front of the hole. Daniel walks up to her and hugs her from behind. Valeria points at the hole.

> VALERIA
Richi crawled in there.

> DANIEL
What?

> VALERIA
Chasing a ball . . . he crawled in there.

Daniel looks at the hole.

> DANIEL
He'll probably be out any minute.

> VALERIA
He crawled in five hours ago.

Daniel crouches down and looks in. He gets up.

> DANIEL
What can we do to get him out?
> (*puts his finger to his lip*)
I know.

He goes into the kitchen and comes back with Richi's plate full of chocolates. He puts it into the hole.

I bet that as soon as he smells the chocolates he'll come running.

He gets up and looks at Valeria.

Do you want me to make you an omelet?

She nods. Daniel goes into the kitchen. Valeria sits motionless.

> DANIEL (O.S.)
> Richi is fine. He may be a little lost, but he's in the apartment. He's not in the street, they haven't stolen him, he's here with us, OK?

INT. APARTMENT — NIGHT

Valeria and Daniel are asleep. Suddenly a noise is heard. Valeria sits up. The noise is coming from under her. She turns on the light.

> VALERIA
> Daniel, Daniel . . .

Daniel wakes up, rubbing his eyes.

> DANIEL
> What's up?

> VALERIA
> Shhh, listen . . . it's Richi . . .

We can hear noises under the bed. Daniel gets down and puts his ear to the floor.

> DANIEL
> Yep, it's him . . .

> VALERIA
> What do we do?

> DANIEL
> Wait a second . . .
> (*starts talking to Richi through the floor*)
> Richi, Richi . . .

He slowly crawls toward the living room. The dog can be heard going in that direction. Daniel reaches the living room and looks through the hole. Valeria calls out to him from the room.

Daniel, come here . . .

Daniel goes back.

He's back here again, listen.

The noises can be heard again.

Let me try. Help me.

She moves on to the wheelchair and bends down as far as she can.

Richi, Richi, come here, darling.

Daniel wheels her toward the living room.

Richi, Richi . . .

They reach the hole. Daniel looks in.

DANIEL

No sign of him.

VALERIA

Shh, let's try and hear where he is.

Valeria signals for silence. They are both listening, concentrated, when the phone rings. They both jump.

DANIEL

Hello, hello . . .

Hangs up.

VALERIA

Who was it?

DANIEL

I don't know. They hung up.

Valeria looks at him suspiciously.

FADE OUT.

INT. CHIVO'S HOUSE — NIGHT

El Chivo is sitting in the living room, surrounded by his dogs. Cofi is lying in a corner with a bandage around his side. El Chivo pets him.

INT. ROOM — DAY

Daniel and Valeria are in the room. She is lying on the bed and he is dressing before the mirror.

> VALERIA
> What are you doing today, Pumpkin?

> DANIEL
> I've got an appointment with the photographers at ten, with the stockholders at two and I've got an editorial meeting in the afternoon.

> VALERIA
> Don't go. Stay.

> DANIEL
> I promise that after the magazine's out on the second of May I'll stay with you a lot more.

> VALERIA
> I don't want to stay here alone.

> DANIEL
> That's precisely why I hired Doña Juanita . . . She's a good person, you'll see.

Valeria doesn't look pleased. Daniel kisses her on the mouth.

> Bye, sweetie. I'll be back as soon as I can.

Leaves.

> DANIEL (O.S.)
> I'm off, Doña Juanita. Take care of Valeria.

> JUANITA (O.S.)
> Yes, sir, don't worry.

We hear the door close.

INT. ROOM — DAY

Valeria is in front of the TV. She changes the channels. Juanita is dust-

ing next to her. Valeria gives her an unpleasant look. The phone rings, and Valeria mutes the TV.

VALERIA

Yes.

MANUEL

Hey, darling.

VALERIA

Manuel, you bastard, where've you been?

MANUEL

Oh, you know, working. What about you, how are you doing?

VALERIA

I'm all right. One day at a time.

MANUEL

Take it easy.

VALERIA

If everything works out I can be back with Enchant in a month.

MANUEL

Oh, forget about that.

VALERIA

What do you mean, 'Forget about that'?

MANUEL

Well, yeah, forget it. The people at Enchant cancelled the contract.

VALERIA

They cancelled it?

MANUEL

Sugar, what did you expect with your leg the way it is . . . for them to wait? Look, to tell you the truth . . .

Valeria looks pensive and slowly hangs up the phone while Manuel's voice is heard. Juanita looks at her curiously. Valeria looks at her in silence. She turns the volume on again.

INT. LIVING ROOM – DAY

Valeria is in the living room, reading a magazine. Juanita walks up behind her.

JUANITA
See you tomorrow, ma'am . . .

VALERIA
Goodbye.

Doña Juanita leaves. Valeria moves toward the hole in her wheelchair. She stops, gets out of the chair, walks two steps and bends down. She finds that half the chocolates have bite marks.

You little bastard!

She listens closely and hears some faint noises. She gets back into her chair and goes to get a flashlight from a chest of drawers. She goes back to the hole, bends down and shines the light into the hole.

Richi, Richi . . .

She sees something move. She moves the flashlight and spots an enormous rat. She screams, gets up and runs to the wheelchair. She sits down and winces in pain.

INT. CONFERENCE ROOM – DAY

Daniel is in the conference room with a man and a woman. They are going over some layouts.

DANIEL
Why don't you raise the picture and lower the text?

WOMAN
No, the composition is unbalanced.

MAN
What if we move it over to the right?

A secretary interrupts them.

SECRETARY
Mr Estrada, you have a phone call.

DANIEL

Tell them to leave their number and I'll call them back.

SECRETARY

It's urgent. I think it's your wife.

INT. OFFICE — DAY

He sits down at his desk and picks up the phone.

DANIEL

What's up, Julieta?

(*no answer*)

Julieta, talk to me . . .

VALERIA

I'm not Julieta.

DANIEL

Honey, I'm sorry, it's just that the secretary . . .

VALERIA

Why do you need to talk to Julieta?

DANIEL

I don't need to talk to her. It was a mistake.

VALERIA

Why do you have to talk to her?

DANIEL

I told you, I don't have to.

VALERIA

So?

DANIEL

Valeria, you're never like this. What's the matter?

(*pause*)

Sweetie?

VALERIA

(*in a broken voice*)

The rats ate Richi.

DANIEL

What rats?

INT. APARTMENT — NIGHT

Valeria is sitting on her wheelchair, staring at the hole in distress.

VALERIA

There are thousands of rats down there.

DANIEL

How do you know?

Valeria shows him the flashlight. Daniel takes it and bends down to take a look.

VALERIA

I saw them. I'm sure they ate Richi.

DANIEL

Rats don't eat dogs. Dogs won't let them: they bite them.

VALERIA

Not if there are thousands of them.

DANIEL

Then let's set out some rat poison.

VALERIA

No. Richi can get poisoned.

DANIEL

We stick a cat in.

VALERIA

He'll fight with Richi.

DANIEL
(*raising his voice*)

Valeria, enough.

Valeria gives him a serious look. Her eyes start to get teary. Daniel moves his hands without knowing what to say. He bends down beside her.

I'm sorry, honey. Everything'll be all right, you'll see.

Valeria looks up at him angrily.

> VALERIA

Sure, that's easy for you to say. Look at me: I'm going to be covered in scars.

> DANIEL
> (*trying to keep calm*)

Plastic surgery has come a long way, honey. Every scar will barely be a little line.

> VALERIA
> (*screaming*)

You're lying . . . you're lying . . .

She's desperate. Daniel is about to say something when a bark is heard below the floor.

> DANIEL

Listen, listen . . .

> VALERIA
> (*eyes lighting up*)

It's Richi . . .

> DANIEL

Yes, he must have heard your shouting. Keep shouting . . .

> VALERIA
> (*screaming*)

Richi, come here, boy.

The barking gets closer. Daniel and Valeria get excited, but we hear Richi go past the hole. Valeria sighs, disappointed. Daniel goes into the kitchen, comes out with a hammer and starts banging the floor around the hole.

> DANIEL

Let's see if he comes out if I make the hole bigger.

He sweats. He's having a hard time ripping up the floor.

> VALERIA

Won't the rats get out?

DANIEL

If they didn't come out before, I don't see why they'll come out now.

He makes the hole larger and peers in.

I don't think that's enough. Let's see: call him.

VALERIA

Richi, Richi . . .

The barking is heard again. Valeria keeps calling him. Suddenly the phone rings. Valeria answers.

Yes, hello . . .

(*slams down the receiver*)

Fuck you.

(*turns to Daniel*)

Who hung up on me?

DANIEL

I have no idea.

VALERIA

When I called and hung up, you knew it was me. Who was it?

DANIEL

I told you, I don't know, OK?

Valeria gives him a questioning look.

EXT. GARDEN – NIGHT

El Chivo is in his garden. Cofi is behind him. He stares at the flames from a pyre. The fire lights his face up. He seems afflicted.

INT. DANIEL'S OFFICE – DAY

Daniel and Andrés are sitting before a large computer screen. The magazine cover with Andrés' photograph is on it.

ANDRÉS

Do I look old?

DANIEL

No, you are old.

Andrés leans back in his chair. He seems displeased.

ANDRÉS

You wish you looked as good as I do for half an hour.

Daniel laughs mockingly.

DANIEL

All right, kid, let's go. It's late.

They get up and head toward the door.

INT. HALLWAY — DAY

Both walk down the hall.

ANDRÉS

How's Valeria?

DANIEL

Sometimes good, sometimes bad . . . she gets angry, she gets bored . . .

ANDRÉS

Doesn't she have anyone to visit her?

Daniel shakes his head.

What about her friends?

DANIEL

Ailing models don't have friends.

ANDRÉS

True, true. What about her family?

DANIEL

Her mother died and her father won't talk to her; he says modeling is a whore's job.

ANDRÉS

Nice father-in-law you've got there. Well, why don't you hire her a nurse?

DANIEL

She can barely stand the maid. Besides, I'm pretty low on cash. The apartment and the hospital have me damn near broke.

ANDRÉS

Didn't Valeria have any savings?

DANIEL

No, God dammit. And to make things worse neither Valeria nor the car were insured.

ANDRÉS

Are you going to stay with her once she gets better?

Daniel looks at him and doesn't answer.

INT. ROOM – NIGHT

Daniel is asleep. Valeria is not in bed. Daniel rolls over and wakes up when he doesn't feel her. He goes into the living room.

INT. LIVING ROOM – NIGHT

Valeria is sitting in her wheelchair, looking at her billboard.

DANIEL

Valeria, what's wrong, sweetheart?

She turns and cries quietly. Daniel walks up to her. He touches her cheek and turns her toward him.

What's wrong?

VALERIA

My leg hurts. I can't take it any more.

DANIEL

I'll take you to the hospital right now, if you want.

VALERIA

No, no. I already spoke to the doctor and he said it's normal that my leg should hurt every now and then. But I feel terrible, like my leg is going to explode.

82

DANIEL

Did he send you any medicine?

VALERIA

Yes, anti-inflammatory pills and painkillers. He told me to call him if it still hurt.

DANIEL

What do you want me to do?

VALERIA

Hold me.

They hug and kiss.

FADE OUT.

INT. ROOM – DAY

Valeria is in front of the TV. She changes the channels repeatedly.

INT. KITCHEN – DAY

Valeria is in the kitchen in front of the cupboard. She is in her wheelchair looking at the sugar bowl and coffee. She stretches to reach it and can't.

Juanita walks in and tries to help her, but Valeria glares at her. Valeria stands up, brings down the sugar bowl and the coffee, and sits down again, holding in the pain, proud.

INT. LIVING ROOM – DAY

Valeria is sitting next to the hole, reading fashion magazines. She hears a noise. She shines the light down the hole: a rat caught in a rat-trap. The phone rings; she doesn't answer.

FADE OUT.

INT. LIVING ROOM – DAY

Daniel arrives home. Valeria is sitting by the hole with a book.

DANIEL

How are you, honey?

He hugs her and kisses her neck. She turns on the flashlight and points it at the hole. The light shines on the crushed rat.

VALERIA

That's three.

DANIEL

There are more than I thought.

He takes his jacket off and hangs it on a chair.

What about Richi?

VALERIA

At about eleven he barked under our room, at one in the kitchen and a while ago he was in the hall. Why do the rats know where the hole is and Richi doesn't?

DANIEL

Because Richi's new down there.
(bends down, looks in the hole, gets up)
Where's Doña Juanita?

VALERIA

I fired her.

DANIEL

What?

VALERIA

I don't like strangers in my house.

DANIEL

Valeria, who's going to help you now?

VALERIA

I don't need anybody to help me.

DANIEL

Nobody? Who's going to iron, clean, cook? Who the fuck is going to get that rat out of there? Or what, are we going to let it rot?

He puts his hands on his head, upset. He breathes deeply.

I have to make myself something to eat; I have to be out of here by four.

                    VALERIA
But you just got in.

                    DANIEL
I told the girls I'd take them to the park.

                    VALERIA
Don't go.

                    DANIEL
I have to go. They need to see me.

                    VALERIA
I need you more. My leg hurts.

                    DANIEL
I thought you didn't need anyone. Besides, I can't just ditch them, they're my daughters.

                    VALERIA
But you could ditch our son, couldn't you?

                    DANIEL
Valeria, please . . . that was your decision, I didn't force you to do anything. You were the one that didn't want to have it.

                    VALERIA
I could never count on you.

                    DANIEL
You could always count on me – I'm here with you in this apartment.

                    VALERIA
Yeah, sure, thanks for the favor.

Her eyes brim with tears. She turns her chair around and rolls away.

EXT. PARK – DAY

Daniel is sitting on a bench while his daughters ride their bicycles. He looks pensive, worried. Lina drives by him with her hands off the crossbar.

LINA

Look, Dad, no hands . . .

JIMENA

Me too, look . . .

She does the same. Daniel smiles at her and immediately returns to his pondering. The girls ride away. Daniel gets up, goes to a payphone and dials. No answer.

INT. VALERIA'S APARTMENT – DAY

We hear the phone ring. Valeria looks at it without answering.

EXT. PARK – DAY

Daniel tries again. Nothing. He goes back to the bench. His daughters ride by him.

JIMENA

We're going to have a race – can you do the countdown?

Lina and Jimena roll up to an imaginary starting line. Daniel does not count. It is as if he were not there.

Dad, can you count to three?

Daniel seems to wake up from his reverie.

DANIEL

No, we have to go.

LINA

But we just got here.

DANIEL

I've got things to do. Let's go.

The girls look at him, estranged. They get off their bicycles and walk next to their father toward the exit.

EXT. BANK PARKING LOT – EVENING

El Jaibo and Ramiro are inside the Volkswagen. A Bital bank is in the background. Jaibo pulls out a ski mask and starts putting it on.

RAMIRO

What the fuck are you doing?

JAIBO

What do you mean, 'What the fuck am I doing'? I'm putting it on.

RAMIRO

Don't be fucking stupid. Why don't you just stick a sign on that says, 'I'm going to rob a bank.' You rob banks clean, with nothing on.

JAIBO

If you say so.

Ramiro pulls out the clip from his pistol and puts it back in.

INT. BANK – EVENING

Leonardo – a fifty-seven-year-old man with a trimmed mustache, shaved gray hair, cashmere pants and a leather jacket – walks in with a young twenty-seven-year-old also with short hair, dressed in jeans and a leather jacket. Leonardo points out the entrance.

LEONARDO

Wait for me here. I'm just going to cash a check.

He steps into the queue while the other man rests at the door. Ramiro and Jaibo walk in and get into separate queues. Suddenly Ramiro and Jaibo pull out their guns.

RAMIRO

Everybody stop, this is a robbery.

A woman screams.

JAIBO

Shut up, bitch.

El Jaibo has the security guard held up. Ramiro goes up to a cashier – the same one that was cashing Leonardo's check.

RAMIRO

Put all the money in a bag. Now.

While she does so, Ramiro makes everyone get on the floor.

Everybody down.

Everyone drops to the floor except Leonardo, who stays on his feet with his hands behind his head.

What wrong with you, asshole?

Leonardo doesn't answer. Ramiro points the gun at him.

Give me your wallet . . .

Leonardo signals that it is in his pocket.

Pull it out.

LEONARDO

You pull it out.

Ramiro removes a black wallet. He opens it and sees a special-agent police ID. Ramiro, surprised, looks up at him. Leonardo raises his eyebrows and laughs mockingly. Suddenly a blast is heard and Ramiro drops to the floor with a shot to the head.

The man who stayed outside the bank is pointing his gun. El Jaibo looks on, frightened and begins to run away. The policeman shouts.

SPECIAL AGENT

Stop, police.

EL Jaibo stops and drops his gun. Ramiro remains on the floor, limp, bleeding.

INT. EXAMINING ROOM – DAY

Valeria is sitting on an examining table with her left leg outstretched. She seems nervous. Daniel holds her hand. The doctor starts removing the bandages.

DOCTOR

I'm going to cut a bit off. Tell me if it hurts.

Valeria winces. Daniel kisses her forehead. As the doctor cuts through the bandage, we see her flesh is swollen, bruised and covered in massive stitches. Daniel is shocked at the sight.

Hmmm, hmmm. I'm going to apply a little bit of pressure.
>> (*looks at the leg, worried*)

Did you walk?

Valeria nods. The doctor cuts some more and cleans the wound. Valeria groans. The doctor continues the check-up. His face is grave.

>> (*to Daniel*)

Did you bring the MRIs?

Daniel hands them over. The doctor looks at them against the light. He seems worried.

All right, Valeria, you can get dressed now.
>> (*to the nurse*)

Help her, Margarita.

The doctor walks out and takes Daniel with him.

Come on. We're crowding the room.

He takes him into his office.

INT. DOCTOR'S OFFICE — DAY

>> DANIEL

It's bad, isn't it?

The doctor nods.

Is that what the scars will look like?

>> DOCTOR

That or worse. Her skin tends to swell.

>> DANIEL

What about plastic surgery?

>> DOCTOR

Not an option. Valeria is not reacting the way I'd hoped she would. If this progresses I'm going to have to operate again.

>> DANIEL

What's wrong with her?

DOCTOR

Let's give it some time.

INT. CAR – DAY

Dusk. Daniel drives. Valeria looks out the window, sad and worried. They do not speak. They stop at a red light.

DANIEL

Do you want to get some sushi or rent a movie?

VALERIA

I'm not in the mood. I don't feel well.

DANIEL

Don't worry, everything is going to be all right.

VALERIA

God dammit! Don't you know how to say anything else?

INT. ROOM – NIGHT

Valeria and Daniel sleep. Suddenly, whining can be heard under the floor. Valeria opens her eyes and turns her bedside lamp on.

VALERIA

Daniel . . . Daniel . . . it's Richi.

Daniel sits up. Valeria gesticulates desperately.

It's Richi – he's crying. Listen: he's crying.

The dog is whining in pain. Valeria struggles to sit up and does so in pain.

Get him out. You've got to get him out.

DANIEL

(*sleepy*)

How?

VALERIA

Rip the fucking floor up if you have to, but get him out! He's dying.

The whines are increasingly pitiful.

DANIEL

I can't rip up the floor; I don't have money to fix it.

VALERIA

Who gives a shit about money?

DANIEL

I do. Right now, a lot more than you can imagine.

VALERIA

Get him out, God dammit . . .

DANIEL

Let him get out by himself.

VALERIA

You selfish bastard, you've always been selfish . . .

DANIEL

How can you say that after I dropped everything for you.

VALERIA

You dropped everything because Julieta was a stupid bitch and your daughters were a couple of brats.

DANIEL

Shut the fuck up – stop talking shit.

VALERIA

I will not shut up.

The dog still howls. Daniel starts stomping on the noise.

DANIEL

Shut your fucking dog up too.

VALERIA

You fucking asshole!

DANIEL

Fuck you, bitch!

Daniel grabs the comforter, walks out and slams the door.

INT. LIVING ROOM — NIGHT

Daniel is in the dark living room. He is sitting on the sofa, looking at the billboard through the open window. He seems crushed. The dog's whining continues, distant and unrelenting.

INT. APARTMENT — DAY

Valeria is sitting in the dining room, drinking coffee. Daniel walks out of the room, briefcase in hand.

> DANIEL
>
> I'll be back for lunch at two.

> VALERIA
> (*aggressive*)
>
> Don't come back for all I care.

> DANIEL
>
> If you say so.

INT. OFFICE — DAY

Daniel is sitting in his office, pensive. He picks up the phone and dials.

INT. JULIETA'S HOUSE — DAY

> JULIETA
>
> Hello, hello . . .

INT. DANIEL'S OFFICE — DAY

Daniel listens to his ex-wife on the line. He slowly hangs up and takes a deep breath.

INT. APARTMENT — NIGHT

Daniel walks in with the same clothes from the previous scene. He puts his briefcase on the dining-room table. He walks toward the room. On the way he discovers more attempts at making holes in the floor. It is obvious that Valeria tried to get Richi out by herself. He knocks on the door to his room. It is locked.

DANIEL

Valeria, open up.

Valeria doesn't answer.

Open up.

VALERIA (O.S.)

Leave me alone.

Daniel kicks the door. He goes to the sofa, lies down and covers himself with the comforter.

FADE OUT.

INT. APARTMENT — DAY

Daniel is dressed in the same wrinkled clothes. He knocks on the door. She doesn't answer.

DANIEL

Valeria, open up, let's talk. Valeria, open up, sweetie, we have to talk . . . I've got to change my clothes . . . Valeria . . .

She doesn't answer. Daniel turns around and leaves.

INT. APARTMENT — NIGHT

Daniel arrives home. Again, he leaves his briefcase on the dining-room table. He turns on the lights. The blanket is still on the sofa. He looks into the hole: a rat is caught in the rat-trap, still breathing. Daniel moves toward the room.

DANIEL
(*knocking*)

Valeria, come on, open up, please . . .

She doesn't answer.

I don't have anything to apologize for, but, there: I'm sorry.

She still doesn't answer.

Either you open the door, or I'll open it.

She doesn't answer.

Valeria, I'm warning you: if you don't open the door, I'm going to break it open. One, two, two and one quarter, two and a half, two and three quarters, OK, if this is how you want it: three.

He kicks the door three times and finally manages to knock it down. The unmade bed is empty. He walks around it and finds Valeria lying on the floor she tried to rip up, unconscious.

Valeria, sweetie, what's wrong? Valeria.

He puts his hands on his head. Valeria doesn't answer.

FADE OUT.

INT. HOSPITAL WAITING ROOM – NIGHT

Daniel is in the same waiting room, staring absently. The doctor comes in and sits beside him.

> DANIEL
> (*without looking at him*)

How is she?

> DOCTOR
> (*sighing*)

She had a severe thrombosis that affected the tissue. There would have been less complications had she been found earlier, but she had already sustained a great deal of damage. The muscles weren't irrigated and . . .

> DANIEL

And?

> DOCTOR

The gangrene was already advanced and we had to amputate.

> (*pause*)

I'm very sorry.

FADE OUT.

INT. APARTMENT — NIGHT

Daniel is in the dark, staring at the billboard. He closes the window and goes into the room. He lies down in his clothes. He closes his eyes. A weak whine is heard. He listens carefully. Another one. Daniel sits up and turns on the light. He gets up and puts his ear to the floor. He crawls around until he finds the place where it is coming from.

INT. KITCHEN — NIGHT

He runs into the kitchen. He pulls out rolling pins, an icepick and finally finds an enormous butcher's knife.

INT. ROOM — NIGHT

He goes back into the room and starts banging the floor furiously. He finally breaks it. He only finds a scurrying rat. He makes another hole and, like a madman, another one until he finds Richi. He picks him up. The dog can barely move. He hugs it and sits down on the floor.

    FADE OUT.

INT. APARTMENT — DAY

Daniel wheels Valeria into the apartment. A sheet covers the amputated leg. The air is heavy with sorrow.

Through the window, Valeria sees her billboard has been removed. She turns her chair around to look at the blank wall. Daniel tries to turn her around, but she signals him not to. Daniel hugs her from behind and kisses her. The phone rings.

    FADE OUT.

TITLES OVER BLACK: 'BLACK DOG'

SFX: Telephone ringing over black screen.

INT. S.U.V — DAY

Gustavo — a well-dressed thirty-year-old with a gray suit, blue tie and gelled hair — and Leonardo ride in a Grand Cherokee. Gustavo answers a cell-phone.

GUSTAVO

Hello . . . yeah . . . tell him three o'clock and cancel the other
one, OK?

Hangs up. Leonardo points at the cell-phone.

LEONARDO

When we reach my friend's house, turn that piece of shit off.
He hates them.

Gustavo puts it away. He turns to look at a bag lying on the back seat.

GUSTAVO

What do we need forty sandwiches for?

LEONARDO

As a gesture to my friend, OK?

GUSTAVO

Are you sure he'll do a good job?

LEONARDO

I've told you twenty times already: yes.

GUSTAVO

So what, this friend of yours, is he also a cop?

LEONARDO

No, he's a guy who was in jail for about twenty years.

GUSTAVO

What did he do?

LEONARDO

He was a guerrilla.

GUSTAVO

Like the Zapatistas?

LEONARDO

Yeah, but he was a real son of a bitch. He put a bomb in a
shopping mall, kidnapped a business man, murdered some
cops . . . Make a right here . . .

Gustavo makes a right.

Everyone was after him: the troops, hired guards, the cops, and do you know who got him?

GUSTAVO

Who?

LEONARDO

You're looking at him . . . I caught him peeing in a restaurant. How d'you like that?

Both laugh. Gustavo seems nervous. The cell-phone rings again.

GUSTAVO

Hello, no . . . deposit that check in my account; I'll transfer it . . . yeah . . . bye.

Annoyed, Leonardo scrutinizes him while he reads a tabloid. Gustavo hangs up.

When we get there, what do I say?

LEONARDO

Nothing. I'll take care of business. Whatever you do, don't ask him any personal questions, not one . . .

GUSTAVO

Why?

LEONARDO

Because it pisses him off. Look: he was a normal guy, like you and me, some private university teacher. One day he ups and leaves his wife and daughter and runs off to join the guerrillas.

GUSTAVO

What did they do?

LEONARDO

What were they supposed to do? They went on with their lives. His wife remarried and his daughter . . . I think his daughter doesn't even know he exists. The point is that when he got out of jail something snapped. I found him in the street one day like a stray dog, a wino, can you fucking believe it? I took pity on him and helped him out with some

97

money, found him a place to live and we even became friends. Then he started doing jobs for me.

GUSTAVO

Jobs . . . like this one?

LEONARDO

Yeah, like this one.

The cell-phone rings again. Leonardo points at it.

Gimme – I'll answer.

Gustavo gives it to him. Leonardo throws it out the window.

GUSTAVO

Why did you do that?

LEONARDO

You can buy yourself another one later, man.

EXT. STREET – DAY

They reach a working-class neighborhood and park in front of a low-income house. Behind the black gate is a run-down little garden with overgrown grass. A few cans of dry paint are huddled in a corner. The walls are peeling.

They get out, taking the sandwiches, and ring the bell. No one opens. They ring again and, after a short while, el Chivo opens the door. He looks sleepy. One of his dogs appears behind him.

LEONARDO

Hey, Chivo.

CHIVO
(*in a low growl*)
Hey, Leonardo, what's up?

El Chivo opens the door and greets them in a strangely cordial fashion, as if he were thinking of something else.

LEONARDO

Let me introduce you to a friend of mine: Gustavo Garfias.

El Chivo shakes his hand and squeezes it for a while.

CHIVO

Hey, man.

GUSTAVO
(*cordial*)

Pleased to meet you.

Leonardo gives el Chivo the bags.

LEONARDO

We brought you this.

El Chivo opens the bags and checks them.

CHIVO

Hey, cool, thanks man.

INT. HOUSE – DAY

They go into the house. El Chivo whistles for his dogs, which immediately mill around him. He hands out the sandwiches. The dogs wolf them down. El Chivo opens one up.

CHIVO

No chilli, no onion; cool man, thanks.

He gives one sandwich a bite and asks them to sit down. In the living room are a tattered 'love seat', a wooden chair, a raunchy calendar, and an old turntable. There is a chipped wood and crystal table in the center.

LEONARDO

What happened, did you lose your glasses?

CHIVO

I don't wear them any more: if God wants me to see blurs, let there be blurs.

He laughs stupidly. Gustavo looks nervously at both of them. Leonardo notices and claps Gustavo's knee.

LEONARDO

Give me the picture.

Gustavo puts his hand in his breast pocket and pulls out a photograph.

He gives it to Leonardo.

> *(without letting go of the photograph)*
> My friend Gustavo here needs you to do him a favor.

Leonardo puts the photograph on the table. It is the picture of a handsome, well-dressed, thirty-two-year-old man. El Chivo turns to look at it. One of his dogs, the smallest one, jumps on his lap. El Chivo strokes him.

CHIVO
I don't do this stuff any more, man, I told you last time.

LEONARDO
Gimme a break, are you planning on living off garbage cans again?

CHIVO
Garbage pays off, Leonardo. It really does, look.
> *(lifts his sleeve up and shows off a watch)*
It's a Citizen; I found it in a garbage can. And look at this . . .
> *(shows him a gold ring on his right ring finger)*
. . . also found it.

LEONARDO
Stop bullshitting me, you probably stole them . . .

CHIVO
No, man, they were in the trash . . .

GUSTAVO
> *(interrupting)*
The captain here said you were very good.

Both turn to look at him, surprised at his interjection.

CHIVO
Good at what?

Gustavo gulps and doesn't answer. Leonardo bails him out.

LEONARDO
Help me out here, Chivo. Do the job.

El Chivo takes the photograph and looks at it closely.

CHIVO

Who is he?

GUSTAVO

My partner.

CHIVO

What did he do to you?

GUSTAVO

He's stealing from me.

CHIVO
(*to Leonardo*)

How much is this for?

LEONARDO

50,000 now, 50,000 when you're done.

CHIVO
(*petting his dog*)

100 now, fifty later.

LEONARDO
(*to Gustavo*)

Are you in?

GUSTAVO

All right, but I've only got fifty right now.

Leonardo looks at el Chivo, who nods in approval. Leonardo signals to Gustavo to hand the money over. Gustavo puts the envelope on the table. El Chivo takes it and puts it away without counting it.

CHIVO
(*points at the photograph*)

What's his name?

GUSTAVO

Luis Miranda Solares.

LEONARDO

He lives on Cerro de Maika 1460 and his office is in the Condesa: 29 Amsterdam Street, the penthouse. It's all written behind the photograph.

El Chivo turns the photograph over.

CHIVO

Real blue-collar, isn't he?

He laughs at his joke. The others just smile. El Chivo slaps his knees, puts the dog on the floor and stands up.

We're set, then.

He walks them to the door. Gustavo stops at the threshold.

GUSTAVO

Make it look like a robbery, OK? No people, no trouble.

He looks very nervous. El Chivo squeezes his arm.

CHIVO

Sure, brother: no people, no trouble, no problems.

EXT. STREET — DAY

El Chivo walks down Amsterdam Street followed by his five dogs. He stops at number 29. He sits on the sidewalk and waits. A couple of policemen walk behind him, eye him suspiciously and keep going. El Chivo pulls out a book and starts to read.

EXT. STREET — DAY

Luis Miranda leaves the building with a good-looking thirty-one-year-old woman dressed in a tailor-made suit. El Chivo starts to follow them. Three blocks later, the couple walk into a fancy restaurant. El Chivo looks at them through the windows.

EXT. STREET — DAY

Dusk. El Chivo prowls around the building. He looks tired. Luis Miranda and Gustavo walk out. They talk cheerfully and then say goodbye. Luis heads toward a white Cherokee parked by the opposite sidewalk. He gets in. El Chivo's eyes meet Gustavo's.

EXT. STREET — NIGHT

It's getting dark. El Chivo walks the street followed by his five dogs. He seems to be a lonely, disillusioned man. He walks by Susana and Ramiro. She is carrying the baby and he is carrying a small suitcase. He looks severely beaten.

El Chivo exchanges looks with them and keeps walking. He stops next to a photo booth. He pulls out some coins, puts them in the slot and sits down to have his picture taken.

INT. HOUSE — NIGHT

El Chivo walks into his house followed by his dogs. He goes into the kitchen, opens the refrigerator, takes out a pint of milk and pours himself a glass. He closes the refrigerator and grabs a bottle of rum from a shelf. He pours a considerable amount of rum into the milk and takes a sip.

He sits down at the table and examines the photograph again. One of his dogs jumps on to the chair next to him and starts to drink from his milk. He doesn't mind and alternates sips with the dog.

He pulls out a photograph album from the cupboard. He starts to look through it. There are pictures of him as a young man next to the woman in the picture he stole from the young woman's house, and pictures of her as a girl. He pulls out the photographs he just took and compares them to when he was young. He then takes out some scissors and cuts them out. He sticks one of them on the photograph he stole, in between the woman and the daughter. He sticks the rest in the album, closes it and puts it away.

INT. ROOM — NIGHT

Through the half-open door we see el Chivo in his underwear, lying on his bed. Three of his dogs are lying around the cot. Two of them are licking his feet.

    FADE OUT.

EXT. STREET — DAY

El Chivo pokes around in the garbage. He finds a yo-yo and starts playing with it. Out of the corner of his eye he sees Luis leave the building with the woman in the tailor-made suit. He puts the yo-yo down and grabs his pushcart.

He follows them until they reach another restaurant. He looks at them through the windows and goes on his way. A gold Honda Accord drives by him. A miniature French poodle barks at his dogs. El Chivo looks at the little dog with disdain. The Honda pulls away.

El Chivo is about to cross the street when he hears tires screeching. He turns and sees the exact moment when the Rabbit rams the Honda. He moves toward the accident. A number of curious onlookers have already got there. He nears the Accord. Valeria screams desperately.

VALERIA

Get me out of here, get me out . . .

The onlookers do not move. Valeria is caught in the wreck. She desperately bangs the roof with her bloody hand.

Get me out, get me out.

A traffic policeman tries to calm her down.

POLICEMAN

Try and relax, ma'am, we'll get you out as soon as we can.
(*pushes the onlookers back*)

Move, move.

Valeria howls in pain. Richi barks at the spectators. El Chivo looks in. Valeria's leg is caught in the twisted metal. The policeman pushes El Chivo away.

El Chivo turns around and walks over to the Rabbit. Jorge's body is lying face down beside the car. Two men are trying to get Octavio out. He is badly hurt. El Chivo moves to help them. Octavio is dripping blood and gasping. When he looks into the car, el Chivo realizes that Octavio has a thick bundle of cash and a wallet in his jacket. He turns to the man next to him.

CHIVO

I've got a machete in there.
(*points at the pushcart*)

Go get it.

The man runs off to get the machete. The other man gets up.

MAN 2

I'll go get more help.

He goes. El Chivo tries to help Octavio, who is caught in the steering wheel. He realizes no one is watching and steals the cash and wallet. He quickly hides them in his clothing. Octavio starts choking on his own blood. El Chivo pulls him forcefully and manages to free him. He drags him away from the overturned car and sets him down near the sidewalk. The man comes back with the machete.

MAN 1

Is he still alive?

El Chivo assents. Two ambulances arrive. The paramedics get out. The man calls them.

Over here, over here . . .

Some paramedics run toward Octavio and some toward Valeria. We can still hear her howling. More onlookers start circling the scene. The man gives el Chivo his machete. He takes it in his bloody hands and leaves discreetly.

He leaves the machete in the pushcart and starts cleaning his hands. He suddenly sees Cofi lying three meters away. He is alive but has trouble breathing. No one pays attention to him. El Chivo bends down to check him out. He lifts him up and puts him on the pushcart. The dog tries to bite him, but el Chivo calms him down.

CHIVO

Shhh, shhh . . .

He sets him in the pushcart and leaves with his dogs.

INT. HOUSE — NIGHT

El Chivo is sitting with a bottle of whisky on his lap. He stares at Cofi, lying on a mat, surrounded by his other dogs. Cofi looks very weak.

El Chivo finds the bullet wound and crouches to examine it. He puts his finger in the hole. Cofi groans. El Chivo pours some whisky on the wound. The dog arches in pain, and el Chivo calms him down by patting him on the head until Cofi is limp again.

He sits down again and pulls out the bundle of cash he stole. He counts it twice, slightly surprised. He then takes out the wallet and empties it. It is full of paper, notes. He finds some photographs. One of them has Susana with the baby. Another one has a younger Octavio with his mother and Ramiro. El Chivo puts his glasses on and looks at them carefully.

INT. YOUNG WOMAN'S HOUSE – DAY

The young woman is cleaning up her house. She sees el Chivo through the window. She stops what she is doing and looks at him.

EXT. STREET – DAY

El Chivo turns his head and sees her. They look at each other for a while, and then she slowly closes the curtains. He remains pensive.

EXT. CEMETERY – DAY

El Chivo is standing near a fresh grave (the same one as seen earlier). There is loose earth and withered flowers. He is concentrated. The same woman in her fifties from earlier walks up to him.

> LUISA
> What do you want?

El Chivo looks at her and smiles.

> CHIVO
> Well, you're aggressive.

> LUISA
> Why did you tell me to come here?

> CHIVO
> It's where the dead live, isn't it?

> LUISA
> This is my sister's grave.
> (*points at the grave*)
> If you're going to start with your games, I'm going to leave.

She turns around and starts to walk away. El Chivo stops her.

CHIVO

What are we going to do about Maru?

She turns around and looks at him furiously.

LUISA

About what, Martín? About what?

CHIVO

About telling her the truth.

LUISA

You want to tell her the truth?
                    (*laughs sarcastically*)
You really want her to see what you've become. You want her
to know everything you did to her and my sister and I. Is that
what you want?

CHIVO

Whatever – I'm her father, aren't I?

LUISA

For her, her father was Ricardo.

CHIVO

That faggot.

LUISA

Why don't you leave Maru alone?

CHIVO

I repeat: I'm her father, aren't I?

LUISA

How can you say that if you were never with her?

CHIVO

Let's not forget I was locked away in jail.

LUISA

That was your choice.

CHIVO

No, it was for a cause.

Well, look at what happened to you and your cause. If you want your daughter to know the truth, you tell her. I'm not the one to destroy the memories she has of you, but you can do whatever the hell you want.

She turns around and leaves. El Chivo shouts at her.

CHIVO

I'm alive, Luisa, more than ever.

She turns and looks at him contemptuously.

INT. CHIVO'S HOUSE — DAY

El Chivo walks downstairs. His five dogs happily surround him. El Chivo walks toward Cofi, who is lying down, and pets him. El Chivo goes to the door. His dogs try to follow him, but he slams the door before they can. The smallest dog desperately scratches the door while another one barks.

EXT. HOUSE — DAY

El Chivo goes into the garage and takes the plastic cover off a 1965 Valiant. He gets in and tries to start it. The car chokes. After a few tries he manages to start the car and leaves.

EXT. STREET — DAY

El Chivo stakes out the entrance to the building. Luis walks out with the good-looking woman. They get into the Cherokee. El Chivo gets into his car and follows them for a few blocks until they drive into a motel. He watches how someone waits on them and leads them into a curtained driveway. He parks.

EXT. STREET — DAY

Dusk. Luis parks on a tree-lined avenue. He and the woman say good-bye. She gets out, looks about her and walks into a luxurious apartment building. Luis starts the car, and el Chivo follows him.

EXT. STREET — NIGHT

It is getting dark. Luis parks next to a small shop and gets out. El Chivo parks a few meters behind him.

INT. VALIANT — NIGHT

El Chivo loads the gun and hides it in his jacket. He gets out of the car.

EXT. STREET — NIGHT

Some distance away, he sees Luis ask the attendant for something. He pays, leaves the shop and walks toward his S.U.V. El Chivo walks toward him decisively. He squeezes the gun and slowly starts to pull it out. Just when el Chivo seems ready to kill him, two children run up to Luis.

> BOY 1
> *(to Luis)*
> I took care of your car, sir.

> BOY 2
> That's not true, I did.

When he sees them, el Chivo plays dumb. He turns around and keeps walking. The children push each other.

INT. CHIVO'S HOUSE — DAY

El Chivo is feeding Cofi, who seems better. He eats heartily. El Chivo strokes him. He gets on his feet and goes to the door. Cofi follows him with the other dogs. El Chivo doesn't let him out and locks him up with all the others.

EXT. STREET — DAY

El Chivo is staking out the building. Suddenly, we hear a ring banging on glass. It is Leonardo in his patrol car. The young policeman from the earlier scene is behind the wheel. They are dressed as they were in that scene.

> CHIVO
> Hey, Leo, what are you doing around here?

LEONARDO

You know, keeping a lookout.
                    (*signals the building with his eyes*)
What's keeping you, Chivo? It's been over a week.

CHIVO

It isn't easy.

LEONARDO

It never is, is it?

CHIVO

Tell your friend to stop whining. I'll be done the day after
tomorrow at the latest.

LEONARDO

All right then, that's your word . . . Anyway, I'm off. I've got
to go cash a check.

He signals the other policeman to keep going. El Chivo watches him go.

EXT. STREET — DAY

*Dusk. El Chivo follows Luis's car in his own. Luis is with the woman.
They go into the motel again. El Chivo slams the steering wheel.*

CHIVO

Jesus Christ, you two are horny!

He keeps driving.

INT. WAKE — NIGHT

*A small group of people is sitting around a coffin. Among them are
Octavio and his mother. He still looks battered: right leg bandaged,
head shaved with a number of cuts on his head, a black eye, forearm in
a cast. There are some crutches beside him. A stranger walks up to
them.*

STRANGER

I'm very sorry, Doña Concha.

MOTHER

Thank you.

The stranger gives her a little hug and leaves. The mother still sits. Suddenly Susana walks in. Octavio notices her, grabs his crutches and laboriously moves toward her. The mother looks at him angrily. Octavio reaches Susana, who looks at him, frightened. They are face to face.

SUSANA
(*nervous*)

How are you?

OCTAVIO

Beat up, but better.

They remain silent. Octavio won't stop looking at her eyes.

Why did you leave?

SUSANA

I don't think this is the time to talk.

OCTAVIO

Then when?

Susana lowers her eyes and walks out of the room into the hallway.

SUSANA

Ramiro was my husband.

OCTAVIO

What about our plans?

SUSANA

You know what my grandmother says? If you want to make God laugh, tell him your plans.

OCTAVIO

You lied to me, Susana.

SUSANA

No, I didn't lie to you. We were lying to ourselves.

OCTAVIO
(*points at the coffin*)
We're not lying to anyone now . . . Stay with me . . .

SUSANA

God dammit, Octavio, I don't know how you can ask me that after everything that's happened! Don't you get it?

OCTAVIO

You're the one that doesn't get it. And it may give God a good laugh, but I'm going on with my plans. Next Sunday, at twelve, I'm going to Ciudad Juárez . . .

SUSANA

You're crazy, Octavio, just look at you . . .

OCTAVIO

I don't give a shit. I'll be waiting for you. You decide if you come or not. Now do you get it?

He turns around to leave.

SUSANA

Ramiro . . .

Octavio turns to look at her, distant.

If it's a boy, I'm calling him Ramiro . . .

Octavio looks at her belly and turns around again.

INT. HOUSE – NIGHT

CHIVO

Well, well, look who's feeling better.

Cofi leans against his leg. El Chivo bends down to look at him and in doing so is stained with blood. El Chivo looks at his reddened hands. He can find no wound.

He stands up and walks into the living room. He finds four of his dogs are dead and the smallest one is hidden underneath the love seat, trembling and bloody. El Chivo looks at one of his dogs: its trachea is torn apart. Cofi follows him wagging his tail. El Chivo pulls out his gun and points it at Cofi. He wags his tail even more. El Chivo cannot shoot him. He puts the gun away, grabs Cofi by the neck and throws him against one of the dead dogs.

No, no, no, bad dog, no . . .

Cofi squirms and tries to get loose. El Chivo strikes him furiously. The dog frees himself and runs to hide in the kitchen. El Chivo bends down to get the little dog out from underneath the love seat. He wraps him in Cofi's towel and walks out.

EXT. STREET – NIGHT

El Chivo goes to the garage, takes the cover off the Valiant, gets in and sets the dog down on the passenger's seat. When he tries to start the car he realizes the dog is already dead. He beats the windshield several times, rabid, sad.

EXT. GARDEN – NIGHT (ENDS ON SAME SHOT AS EARLIER SCENE IN WHICH EL CHIVO IS STARING AT A PYRE)

El Chivo digs a hole in his back yard with a shovel. It is a large hole. Cofi watches. When he's done, el Chivo puts the five dogs in the hole, douses them in gasoline and throws in a lit match. He watches how the flames consume the carcasses.

INT. HOUSE – NIGHT

El Chivo is lying on his cot, face up, staring at the roof. He turns on the light, grabs his glasses, puts them on and looks around him. He turns the light off and keeps looking up at the roof.

FADE OUT.

INT. HOUSE – DAY

El Chivo walks downstairs, followed by Cofi. He pockets a revolver and handcuffs. At the door he turns around and kicks Cofi. The dog runs away. El Chivo leaves.

EXT. STREET/VIDEO RENTAL STORE – DAY

El Chivo watches Luis inside a video store. He sees him check the shelves and rent his film. Luis walks out toward his Grand Cherokee. El Chivo pulls out his gun and hides it in his clothes. He catches up to Luis and sticks the gun in his back discreetly.

CHIVO

Do what I say or I'll kill you.

LUIS
(*over his shoulder*)

All right . . .

CHIVO

Open the passenger door and don't do anything stupid.

Luis opens the passenger door.

Get in slowly, asshole.

Luis gets in and slides over to the driver's seat. El Chivo gets in, still pointing the gun. He pulls out the handcuffs and throws them at Luis.

Put one cuff on your left wrist and the other one on the wheel.

Luis cuffs his left wrist and puts his right hand on the wheel.

No, you moron: cuff yourself to the wheel.

Luis does as he is told.

Start the car and don't even think of looking anywhere other than straight ahead.

Luis starts the car and drives. El Chivo makes sure no one has seen them.

(*points*)

That way.

LUIS

What is this: robbery or kidnapping?

CHIVO

It might be the last day of your life, asshole.

Luis bites his lip. He drives. El Chivo pulls out the photograph of Luis and shows it to him.

I was paid to blow your head off, brother. How about that?

Luis looks at el Chivo, disturbed, and gulps.

EXT. STREET — DAY

The S.U.V. drives through the city streets. Luis parks in front of el Chivo's house.

INT. S.U.V. — DAY

> CHIVO
> *(gives him a key)*
> Take the handcuff off the wheel . . .

Luis does so.

> . . . and put it on your right wrist.

He does so.

> You're going to get out slowly, you hear me, man? I want your hands on your stomach, as if you had a stomach ache. Don't even think of doing something stupid. Get out on my side.

El Chivo gets out of the S.U.V. Luis follows him. Some boys are playing football in the street. Luis looks at them imploringly.

> Watch yourself, man.
> *(shows him the gun)*
> Walk toward the door.

Luis walks in front of el Chivo, who opens the black gate. They walk in. El Chivo opens the door to the house and signals him to walk in. Cofi receives them, wagging his tail.

INT. HOUSE — DAY

El Chivo takes Luis into the living room. He takes the cuff off Luis's left wrist.

> CHIVO
> Sit down on that chair.

Luis obeys.

> Put your hands under the seat.

Luis obeys. El Chivo cuffs his hands under the chair so that he cannot escape. He stands in front of him.

What do you want to drink? I've got rum, milk and water.

LUIS

What are you going to do with me?

CHIVO

What does that mean: rum, milk or water?

LUIS

It means what it means.

El Chivo grabs another wooden chair. He puts the backrest toward Luis and sits down to face him.

CHIVO

I'm offering you something to drink, asshole, and if you were a little bit more perceptive, just a little bit, you'd realize that at least for now I'm not planning on killing you, get it? Now: rum, milk or water?

LUIS

Water.

El Chivo goes into the kitchen. Luis is left alone and tries to break loose. He stops when he sees Cofi looking at him. El Chivo comes back in with a glass of milk in one hand and a glass of water in the other. He puts the glass of water on the floor. He lifts his up and toasts.

CHIVO

Cheers.

LUIS
(*hesitating*)

How am I supposed to drink it?

CHIVO

I may be your waiter, but I'm not your nanny, man.

He sips his milk.

LUIS

Who paid you to kill me?

CHIVO

You can't guess?

LUIS

No.

CHIVO

What if I told you it's that broad you fuck almost every day at the Hotel Florencia?

LUIS
(*surprised*)

Marta? No, it can't be her.

CHIVO

You're right: not her. It was your wife.

LUIS

She knows about Marta?

CHIVO

I don't know, does she?

Luis, confused, breathes agitatedly. El Chivo laughs mockingly.

No, man, it wasn't her either.

LUIS

Marta's husband?

CHIVO

Oh, she's married?

Luis doesn't answer. El Chivo seems amused.

As you can see, a fuckload of people want to kill you.

El Chivo gets up and walks around the living room. Luis watches him anxiously.

(*points at Cofi*)
Would you believe I don't know what my dog's name is? I found him in the street. What would you call him?

LUIS

Stray dog.

CHIVO

Original, man, real original. Why don't we call him . . . Gustavo?

LUIS

Gustavo?

CHIVO

Do you know any Gustavos?

LUIS

My brother's name is Gustavo.

CHIVO

Gustavo Garfias?

LUIS

Gustavo Garfias Solares; he's my half-brother.

CHIVO

Oh, Abel, Abel, Abel! What did you do to deserve a brother like that? He told me you were partners.

LUIS

My brother and my partner. He paid you?

El Chivo nods.

Why?

CHIVO

I don't know. You tell me.

LUIS

How much did he pay you?

CHIVO

5,000 pesos.

LUIS

Five? Five measly fucking thousand pesos?

CHIVO

Well, he also gave me some tickets to the Rolling Stones concert.

LUIS

Fucking faggot piece of shit, I didn't do anything to him.

CHIVO

He said you were ripping him off.

LUIS

That's not true . . . that's not true . . .

CHIVO

Don't get angry, man, that's what he said. And stop yelling because I'm going to have to shoot you to shut you up.
(*points at Cofi again*)
What do we call him then?

LUIS

I don't give a shit about your dog.

CHIVO

Don't talk about my dog like that. If I haven't killed you, it's thanks to him.

El Chivo walks around him. He pulls Luis's chair toward a pillar, gets a rope and starts tying him up from head to toe. When he's done he gets a handkerchief and duct tape. He puts the handkerchief in his mouth and puts tape over it.

I'll be upstairs watching TV. Give me a shout if you want something for dinner.

El Chivo turns the light out and walks upstairs, followed by Cofi.

FADE OUT.

INT. HOUSE — DAY

El Chivo walks downstairs. He seems in a good mood. Cofi follows. He greets Luis.

CHIVO

Morning.

He goes into the kitchen and grabs two bananas. He goes back into the living room and feeds Luis, who has trouble chewing.

LUIS

What are you going to do with me?

119

CHIVO

I don't know, I'll think about it.

LUIS

If you let me go I can give you a lot of money, and if you kill
my brother I'll give you as much of it as you want.

El Chivo pulls out the wad of cash and shows it to him.

CHIVO

Would you believe me if I told you that I don't need it?

*He offers Luis some more banana and some water, which Luis gulps
down.*

I've got to go. I'll be back later.

LUIS

You're just going to leave me here? I need to go to the bathroom.

El Chivo crams the handkerchief in again, followed by the duct tape.

CHIVO

I won't be long.
(*points at Cofi*)
Keep an eye on him for me.

EXT. JUNKYARD — DAY

*El Chivo is with a man in a junkyard. The man gives el Chivo a bun-
dle of cash, which he hides in his jacket pocket. In exchange, el Chivo
gives him the keys to Luis's S.U.V.*

EXT. STREET — DAY

El Chivo is talking on a payphone.

LADY

Plexus, good afternoon . . .

CHIVO

Gustavo Miranda, please.

LADY

May I ask who's calling?

CHIVO

Tell him it's el Chivo and that it's urgent.

LADY

Just a second . . .

Some moronic music is heard. Gustavo answers, nervous.

GUSTAVO

Hello . . .

CHIVO

Do you have my money?

GUSTAVO
(*disturbed*)

Is it done?

CHIVO

Didn't you realize he didn't go to work today?

GUSTAVO

Yeah, it's just that . . .

CHIVO

Bring the money over to my place. Be there in two hours, man. Don't be late.

Hangs up.

EXT. HOUSE – DAY

El Chivo is sitting on the doorstep. He watches Gustavo arrive in his green Cherokee. Gustavo gets out and walks toward him.

CHIVO

Put the club on – they steal a lot of cars around here.

GUSTAVO

I won't be long, will I?

El Chivo smiles and shakes his head. Gustavo opens the black gate and nervously hands over a manila envelope.

Here it is.

El Chivo takes the envelope, gets up and signals Gustavo to come in.

I'd better be going.

CHIVO

Come in.

INT. HOUSE — DAY

They enter. El Chivo locks the door. Gustavo looks at him, frightened.

GUSTAVO

What's wrong? The money's all there.

CHIVO

Nothing's wrong. Come in.

INT. LIVING ROOM — DAY

He leads him into the living room. Gustavo finds Luis gagged and bound. Their eyes bulge in amazement. Gustavo grows pale.

CHIVO

Have you two met?

GUSTAVO

This wasn't the deal.

CHIVO

What was the deal?

GUSTAVO

That you were going to . . .

El Chivo brandishes the gun.

CHIVO

That I was going to do what, man?

GUSTAVO

That you were, that your job was . . .

CHIVO

Well, it wasn't entirely clear to me.

(*cocks the gun*)
You wanted him erased? Well, you erase him.

He gives him the gun. Gustavo grabs it mechanically.

All yours, Cain.

Gustavo looks at him, disconcerted.

Kill him, you pussy.

Luis squirms in his chair. Gustavo doesn't know what to do. El Chivo pushes him toward Luis.

You've got him all to yourself . . .

GUSTAVO
I paid you, I paid you to do this. That was the deal . . .

CHIVO
You're not going to kill him?

Gustavo shakes his head. El Chivo snatches the gun away.

Do you want me to kill him?

Gustavo doesn't answer.

Do-you-want-me-to-kill-him?

Gustavo still doesn't answer. El Chivo holds the gun to Luis's head.

Do I kill him? . . . Answer . . . Do I kill him?

Luis squirms. The shot seems imminent. Gustavo is terrified. El Chivo points the gun at him.

Or better I kill you.

GUSTAVO
No, no, no . . .

CHIVO
(*to Luis*)
Shall I kill him?

Luis nods furiously.

Do you really want me to kill him?

GUSTAVO

No, please, no.

He aims directly at his eyes. Gustavo turns his head.

CHIVO

Stupid fucking yuppie.

El Chivo hits him in the head with the pistol butt. Gustavo falls on his knees and el Chivo hits him again.

FADE OUT.

INT. BATHROOM — DAY

El Chivo is naked, wrapped in a towel. It is obvious that he has just had a shower. His hair is cut and combed. He shaves off his overgrown beard. He wipes the mirror clean and puts on his glasses to get a good look at himself. He smiles.

INT. CHIVO'S ROOM — DAY

El Chivo has a suitcase on his bed. He is well dressed, in a clean shirt and a slightly outdated tweed jacket. He takes a revolver out from one of the drawers and hides it in his pants together with the Browning. He goes downstairs with his suitcase and walks into the living room.

INT. LIVING ROOM — DAY

The two brothers are tied and cuffed to the wooden chairs, facing each other, gagged.

CHIVO

Morning, how'd you sleep?

The brothers look at him like caged animals.

I think you two have a lot to talk about, don't you? It's a shame I can't stay: it would be fascinating. But, you understand, I have to leave town. That's the way this works.

Cofi sits next to el Chivo and he pats his head. He pulls out a key and takes their cuffs off without untying them.

El Chivo searches their jackets. He pulls out a wallet (which he pockets), a memo pad and a gold pen. He takes a cell-phone from Luis.

> Make yourselves at home. I hope you can work out your
> problems. In case you can't work things out by talking . . .

He pulls out the revolver and puts it on the floor between them.

> I'll leave you this so you can better understand each other,
> OK?

He holds up the cell-phone.

> I'll call you later to see how things went.

He grabs his suitcase and walks toward the door. He stops.

> There's milk and eggs in the refrigerator in case you want to
> have breakfast.

He leaves the house, followed by Cofi.

EXT. STREET — DAY

*El Chivo stops in front of the same photo booth as before. He takes Cofi
out of the S.U.V. and gets four pictures taken with him. He combs his
hair meticulously before each photograph.*

INT. S.U.V. — DAY

*He opens the suitcase and pulls out the photo album. He sticks the new
photographs on the last page together with the ones he took earlier.*

EXT. STREET — DAY

*We see the S.U.V. leave. The camera stays on the image of Valeria's bill-
board being removed by an employee. Valeria's silhouette collapses on to
the ground.*

EXT. BUS STATION — DAY

*Octavio is standing in front of a bus that says 'Ciudad Juárez'. He
looks at his watch; Susana doesn't show. The driver calls out to him.*

                    DRIVER
Are you coming or staying?

Octavio shakes his head. The driver closes the door. Octavio watches the bus leave.

EXT. STREET — DAY

El Chivo parks in front of the young woman's house. He gets out carrying the photo album and leaves Cofi in the S.U.V. He walks up to the door, takes out his picklock and opens it.

INT. HOUSE — DAY

El Chivo enters the house. He heads toward the young woman's room and sits on her bed. He grabs the photograph he had taken from the picture frame and puts it back. He is now in the picture. He puts the album on the bed and turns on the answering machine that is on the table.

ANSWERING-MACHINE VOICE
Hi, you've reached 5550-00-72. I can't come to the phone right now but if you leave your message, name and number I'll get back to you as soon as I can. Thanks.

El Chivo starts the machine twice to hear the voice. He memorizes the phone number and dials it on the cell-phone. He seems nervous. The answering-machine voice is heard one more time. When he hears the 'beep', el Chivo gulps and starts to talk.

CHIVO
Maru, honey, this is Martín, your father, your blood father. After all these years I've been dead to you, you probably think that this is a joke, but it isn't: I'm a ghost that's still alive. The last time I saw you was the day of your second birthday and since then I swear there hasn't been a day that goes by that I don't think about you. On the afternoon of the last day I saw you, I held you in my arms and hugged you and asked you to forgive me for what I was about to do. I left to never come back; I left believing there were more important things than you and your mother. I wanted to make this a better world to share with you afterwards. I didn't. I ended up in jail and I was never able to see you again. Your mother and I agreed that she would tell you I was dead. It was my

idea, not hers. I promised her I'd never come looking for you, but I couldn't take it any more: I was dying more than I was already dead. You have no idea how much I've missed you. I'll come back to look for you when I have the courage to look you in the eyes. I . . .

The answering-machine 'beep' goes off.

. . . love you very much, sweetie.

He hangs up and remains pensive. He then takes out the money he was carrying. He leaves it on the bed, takes one last look and leaves.

EXT. JUNKYARD — DAY

We see el Chivo selling the green Cherokee to the same crooked dealer.

> MAN
> (*hands over money*)

110, 120, there.

El Chivo hands over the keys; the man looks at Cofi.

What's your dog called?

> CHIVO
> (*looks at the S.U.V.'s name*)

Cherokee.

A dog appears and Cofi growls at it. El Chivo smacks him on the head.

No, Cherokee, no . . .

EXT. JUNKYARD — DAY

El Chivo leaves the junkyard and starts to walk toward a lonely, open field, followed by Cofi.

EXT. HOUSE — DAY

We see the front of el Chivo's house. Three shots ring out.

FADE OUT.

Octavio (Gael García Bernal) is tended to after the car crash

Susana (Vanessa Bauche)

Ramiro (Marco Pérez)

Octavio (Gael García Bernal)

Jarocho (Gustavo Sánchez Parra)

Daniel (Alvaro Guerrero)

Valeria (Goya Toledo)

El Chivo (Emilio Echevarría)